ACT THERAPY WORKBOOK

for

ANXIETY RELIEF

A Simple Acceptance & Commitment Therapy Toolbox to Help Reduce Stress, Panic Attacks, Worry and Depression

Includes 30+ Mindfulness and Coping Strategies

LIFEZEN PUBLICATIONS

ISBN 9789083397443 (Paperback)
ISBN 9789083397450 (Hardback)

DEDICATION

I wrote this for you.
You deserve relief from your anxiety and pain.

Ava Watters

A Gift to Our Readers!

Get **Emergency Calming Techniques** for free now! Discover **science-backed exercises** designed to bring instant calm during anxiety episodes. (These are extra techniques not included in the book.)

Visit https://life-zen.com/guides/calm or simply scan the QR code on this page.

Table of Contents

Introduction

"Panic attacks feel like you're stuck in a nightmare, and the only escape is to wake up, but you can't." — Unknown

I was 12 years old when I had my first panic attack (at least, that's the one I remember). It was a normal, boring afternoon; I was helping my mom put dishes in the dishwasher when I started feeling really dizzy out of the blue. I stood perfectly still, trying not to throw up, but I could feel my heart racing, and I couldn't catch my breath.

My mom was not the nervous and dramatic type, so instead of fussing over me, she simply asked, "What's wrong?" I said the first thing that came to my head:

Me: I'm scared.
Mom: Of what?
Me: I don't know.

My mom then proceeded to ignore me as if nothing happened. I managed to get a glass of water and sit. My younger brothers were screaming their heads off in the living room, so my mom left the kitchen, and that was that. I can't describe it, but I couldn't forget what I felt. I felt *fear* as if I were shivering inside.

About a year later, I was sitting in the car with my dad when I had another panic attack. He was dropping me off a swimming date with some girlfriends.

Me: Dad...
Dad: Yeah?
Me: I'm... nervous. (I was dizzy, my heart was racing, I was finding it hard to breathe, and I had that feeling again. I was scared and felt cold just beneath my skin.)
Dad: Huh?

Me: I can't... get... out of the car.
Dad: Ava, you're a great swimmer. There's nothing to be scared about, honey.
Me: I...
Dad: Your friends are waiting inside.
Me: Dad...
Dad: Ava!!!

I was startled. I whipped my head around to look at my dad, and oddly enough, although I could see his impatience, focusing on him made me calm down. I managed to get out of the car, and everything was on autopilot.

Go meet friends, walk to the changing rooms, and change clothes. People surrounded me, but I could barely hear them. I jumped into the pool and swam and swam and swam. By the time I got out of the pool, I was exhausted but was back to myself again.

Over the years, I have experienced moments like this. And with each episode, a "secret fear" was building slowly but surely inside me. You see, I knew my family had a history of mental health issues on my mother's side.

Growing up, there were always whispers about my cousin Ellen, who "stayed home all the time." Later, I would learn she had Major Depressive Disorder (MDD). When I was about eight, we visited my grandparents and met Uncle Frank, my mother's oldest brother, for the first time. I remember thinking it was odd to meet an uncle I never heard of before. Later, I would learn that Uncle Frank had schizophrenia. These events scared and scarred me because although my mom never exhibited any signs of mental health problems, I was just always scared I would get them. That's why I never forgot my first panic attack.

For the record, Uncle Frank leads a productive life. He has a job and lives on his own. However, he continues to experience schizophrenic episodes at various stages in his life, usually brought on by severe stress and anxiety.

Looking back, I'd say that my unaddressed fear of developing mental health problems contributed to... well, my mental health problems. (Yep, the irony!)

This unaddressed fear (no one talked about mental health in my family) made me constantly stressed and anxious inside. I had two younger twin brothers who were the center of the family's attention, which led me to develop an intense desire to be "seen." As a result, I became whatever people wanted me to be. I became a master at people-pleasing. However, since I was only ever trying to please others and be seen, I was always afraid that people would find out I was a fraud. This led to my controlling and perfectionist tendencies. And I've been doing all of these—for years.

Of course, one can only keep the façade for so long. I realize now that as each year passed, **I kept piling mental and emotional weight on my shoulders... until I couldn't anymore.**

I found out the hard way that when you live with unaddressed stress and fear and seek nothing but external validation, you lose yourself bit by bit until there's hardly anything left to lose.

It all came to a head when I was in my mid-30s and suffered what I now call "a burnout and a breakdown."

My career was my "cover." As an International Project Manager, I zigged and zagged across the globe, giving the impression that I was successful and that I'm someone who's got it all together. Ha! Inside, I was a wreck.

I felt like I was constantly swinging wildly between arrogance and self-doubt or between brief moments of calm and intense bouts of anxiety. At the slightest problem in my career or personal life, my mind would become an immediate battlefield where the fear of failure and the pressure to maintain my "successful" image waged a relentless war.

One day, while abroad and alone, I suffered another panic attack. (By this time, I was already used to having them now and then.) This time, however, I felt an enormous dark cloud loom over me. My anxiety subsided, but I couldn't shake my melancholy. Right around the third week, I returned to the hotel where I was staying, and as I entered my quiet suite, I started crying—and I couldn't stop. This scared me. Somehow, I knew it was different this time. Inside, I felt like I was drowning.

I don't know how, but **I survived** the three months I was away and returned home. **But I wasn't the same.**

My panic attacks became more frequent, I had this deep, unshakeable sadness, and I felt just bone-deep tired. So I did the best thing I could've ever done—I reached out for help.

I met with a therapist, and over our sessions, we learned that I was going through burnout, which was already at the cusp of a breakdown. And that underlining this condition was **years of unaddressed anxiety**.

I learned that I fit the description of high-functioning anxiety to a T! My people-pleasing, controlling, perfectionistic, and other tendencies all pushed me to overextend myself in every aspect of my life, leaving me incapable of ever taking a freaking break! However, persistent worries about "dropping the ball" (at home and work), always wearing a mask for the outside world, and constant self-doubt had been silently eroding my mental health for years.

To be honest, recognizing this connection was both eye-opening and validating! It explained why I felt so overwhelmed and why my attempts to simply "push through" weren't working.

I'm incredibly grateful for going through therapy. It was what I needed to see and understand what I was going through. However, I sensed that it wasn't enough. I felt something was missing. It was as if I was seeing a glimpse of something, but I couldn't take the next crucial step towards it. Something was blocking me, but I didn't know what. So, I wrapped up my sessions and set out on my own. After some research, I came upon Dr. Marsha Linehan's Dialectical Behavior Therapy (DBT).[1]

DBT taught me a concept called Radical Acceptance[2], which was my healing turning point. Acceptance was the critical step I was missing! (You'll understand what I mean on **page 65**.)

After learning about the benefits of DBT, I was so captivated that I enrolled in Dr. Linehan's DBT Skills certificate course. From that moment on, I've immersed myself in other forms of therapy, such as Mindfulness-Based Stress Reduction Therapy (MSBR), Cognitive Behavioral Therapy (CBT), and Acceptance and Commitment Therapy (ACT).

I learned that while these therapies have similarities, they also significantly differ.

- MSBR focuses on mindfulness to alleviate stress,
- DBT emphasizes mental and emotional skills training to instigate change,
- CBT focuses on identifying and challenging negative thought patterns to modify behavior, and
- ACT emphasizes acceptance and values-based behavior to improve mental and emotional resilience.

This book is a non-technical (no jargon!), easy-to-understand, and compassionate guide to help you explore and apply ACT for anxiety relief. I'll share with you how ACT helped me accept my anxious thoughts (rather than deny, ignore, or bury them as I have been doing for years). I'll also share with you how ACT helped me develop *psychological flexibility*, which enables me to bounce back better and faster from anxiety episodes.

You'll also discover how ACT helped me live a happier life. I learned that **unhappiness is usually due to a mismatch between what we're doing and what's truly important to us.** This is exactly what I've been doing for years(!), and on **page 109**, I'll guide you on how to finally live the life YOU want (not the life based on what family or society dictates). This was crucial to my healing, and I hope it does the same for you.

When I started my journey, I just wanted to feel better and get some relief from my anxiety. I never thought I was going on this wonderful journey of self-discovery, healing, and transformation. **Today, I don't just feel better, I'm happy.**

Happiness has this way of radiating from you, and the people around me certainly saw the difference. It all started at a BBQ party one summer evening...

One of my best friends had round, wide eyes when she saw me enter their backyard with my husband. Later that evening, she asked:

Friend: Ava, what have you been doing? You look amazing!
Me: Thanks! I feel amazing. And you know I haven't been for a long time.
Friend: I know, but I'm glad to see you this way. What happened? What did you do?

I shared the story of my healing journey for the first time that night. As more saw me, asked me, and reached out, I felt that the best way to live my life was to try to pass on what I'd learned.

So, dear reader, this book is my personal invitation to you to go on a healing journey with me and find relief from anxiety. Together, we'll explore the steps and practices that helped me, hoping they will bring you the same sense of peace and well-being.

How is This Workbook Different?

This book is your simple, modern-day, and "usable in real life" guide to Acceptance and Commitment Therapy (ACT). However, I have a confession: this book is NOT limited to ACT. I've included certain aspects of MSBR, DBT, and CBT that I believe are important in dealing with anxiety. These elements have been important to my healing, and I hope they benefit you, too.

How to Use This Workbook

The chapters in this book build upon one another. Please start from the beginning and work your way through.

Also, I believe that learning is information + action. Simply knowing something isn't enough; you must put what you learn into practice for it to truly make a difference. That's why each chapter in this book includes practical, self-guided exercises. These activities are key to turning the knowledge you get in this book into real-world skills. This hands-on approach is where true transformation takes place.

Content Warning

We'll be tackling anxiety in detail, and some of the real-life stories, topics, and exercises here may trigger you. Stress, distress, loss, conflict, trauma (past and recent), health problems, etc., are examples of such content. Please be aware of these and other topics that may concern you. Also, never hesitate to ask for help or consult a specialist if you feel overwhelmed.

Safety While Reading

Working through anxiety can sometimes get intense, so it's important to take steps to ensure you feel safe and comfortable while engaging with the content. Here are some tips to help:

- **Create a Safe Space.** Find a place where you feel at ease, like a cozy chair or a quiet spot in your home. Choose a place that feels safe, peaceful, and secure.

- **Set Reading Boundaries.** As you read and do the exercises, take breaks when needed and stop if you start feeling overwhelmed. Your well-being comes first.

- **Practice Self-Care.** Take care of your physical and emotional needs. Get enough sleep, eat well, stay hydrated, and do activities that make you happy and relaxed.

- **Create a Safety Plan.** Know what to do if you feel unsafe or overwhelmed. Some ideas:

    - Stop and take a break.
    - Call or message a friend or family member.
    - Go to a safe, calm place.
    - Listen to soothing music or watch something comforting or funny.

Lastly, as you go through this journey, please **always extend patience and kindness to yourself** because this will not be a linear process. Just like me, you'll face ups and downs, but I promise you: If you stick with the process, you'll always move forward.

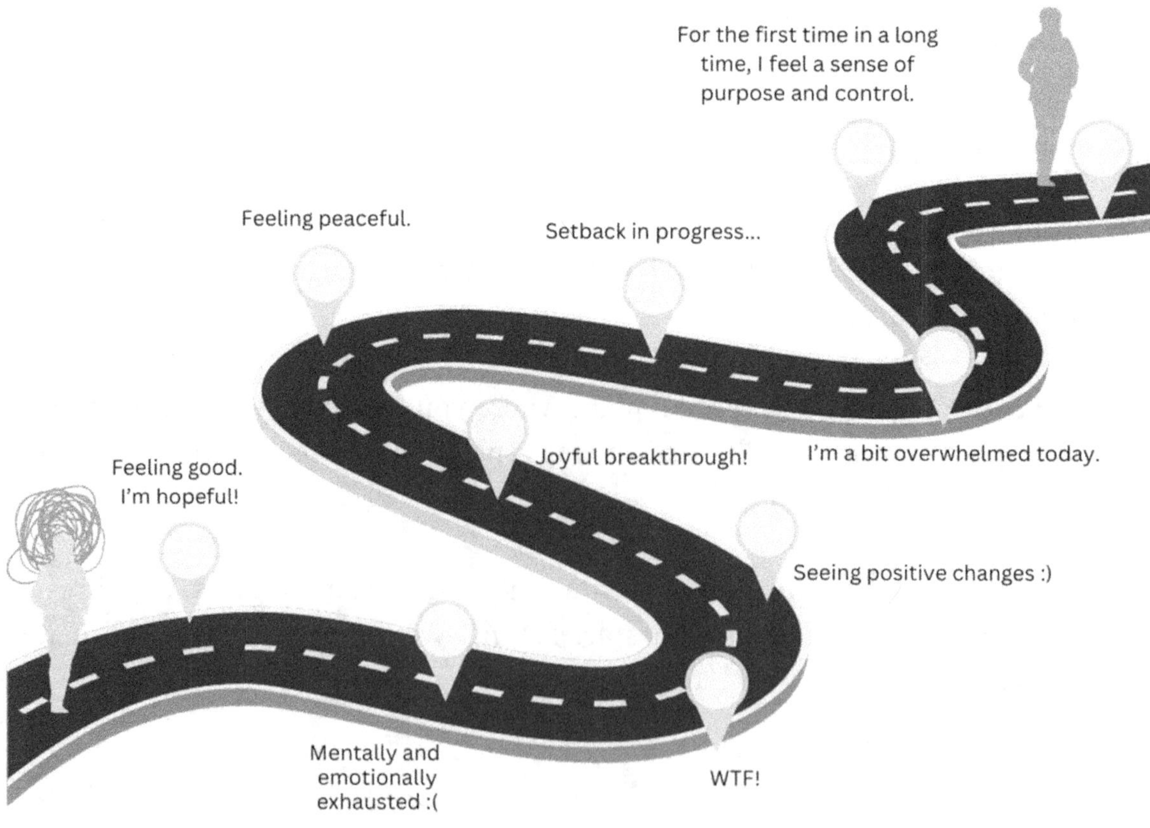

Living with Intention

Living with intention entails making conscious decisions. Life doesn't just happen to us. We have tremendous power and influence over what happens in our lives. So, I ask you now to set your intention, whether that's as simple as, "I intend to finish one chapter a day and do at least one of the exercises in this book" to more profound goals such as, "I intend to embrace this journey, including all its ups and downs, and take proactive steps towards managing my anxiety."

Please set your intention:

____

____

____

____

____

You Matter.

Throughout this journey, please remember that you matter. Your experiences, feelings, and struggles are valid. And your desire for anxiety relief and a better life isn't just important; it's your right.

Also, you're not alone. I have walked a similar path. So, know that YOU HAVE IT IN YOU to manage your anxiety—and transform. Remember, too, to celebrate your progress, no matter how small, because each tiny win is exactly that—a win!

Ava Watters

Amazon Bestselling Author
Acceptance Therapy Advocate

Chapter 1: Understanding Anxiety

"It is very hard to explain to people who have never known severe depression or anxiety the sheer continuous intensity of it. There is no off switch." – Matt Haig

What is Anxiety?

Anxiety is a feeling of worry or fear about what *might* happen in the future. It's like your brain is always looking for danger, even when no real danger is around.

Everyone feels anxious sometimes, like before a big interview or project or when trying something new. But if you often feel anxious, and it hinders you from doing things you want or need to do, then it becomes a problem.

Anxiety can make your heart race, your palms sweat, and your stomach feel upset. It can also make you feel restless, tired, or unable to concentrate. It's like an alarm system in your body that's a bit too sensitive, going off even when there's no real threat.

Anxiety and the Brain

What most people don't understand about anxiety is that it's not just something you *feel*; it affects how the brain works, especially in regions that handle threat response and stress management. When anxiety kicks in, it can cause some areas of the brain to become hyperactive while slowing down others. Here's a basic description of how this all happens.

- The **amygdala** acts as the brain's alarm system and emotion hub. When you sense a threat, it kicks into high gear, triggering feelings of anxiety. For people with anxiety disorders, the amygdala can be overly sensitive, reacting to situations that aren't truly dangerous or even present. This over-activity can lead to intense fear and anxiety, even in non-threatening situations. (Amygdala: "Ooh, threat. Danger! Danger!")

- The **hypothalamus** acts as a command center, managing your body's response to stress. So, when the amygdala detects a threat, it alerts the hypothalamus. The hypothalamus then activates the fight-or-flight response, releasing stress hormones like adrenaline and cortisol. These hormones prepare your body to react to the threat. (Hypothalamus: "There's danger? Pump out the stress hormones!")

- The **prefrontal cortex** is crucial for decision-making, attention, and emotion regulation. However, when anxiety levels are high, this part of the brain can struggle, making it difficult to think clearly, make decisions, and keep emotions in check. This can make anxiety feel overwhelming and difficult to manage. (Other people's prefrontal cortex: "Okay, I've checked. There's no real threat. Calm down." Anxious person's prefrontal cortex: "OH.MY.GOD! What's going on? What should I do? What should I not do? Argh!!!!")

- The **hippocampus** helps with forming memories and regulating emotions. Long-term or chronic anxiety can affect the hippocampus, leading to problems with memory and emotional regulation. This disruption can make it challenging to differentiate between real and imagined threats, worsening anxiety. (Hippocampus: "Wait, is this a real danger or just my imagination? I'm not sure, but let's stay on high alert just in case.")

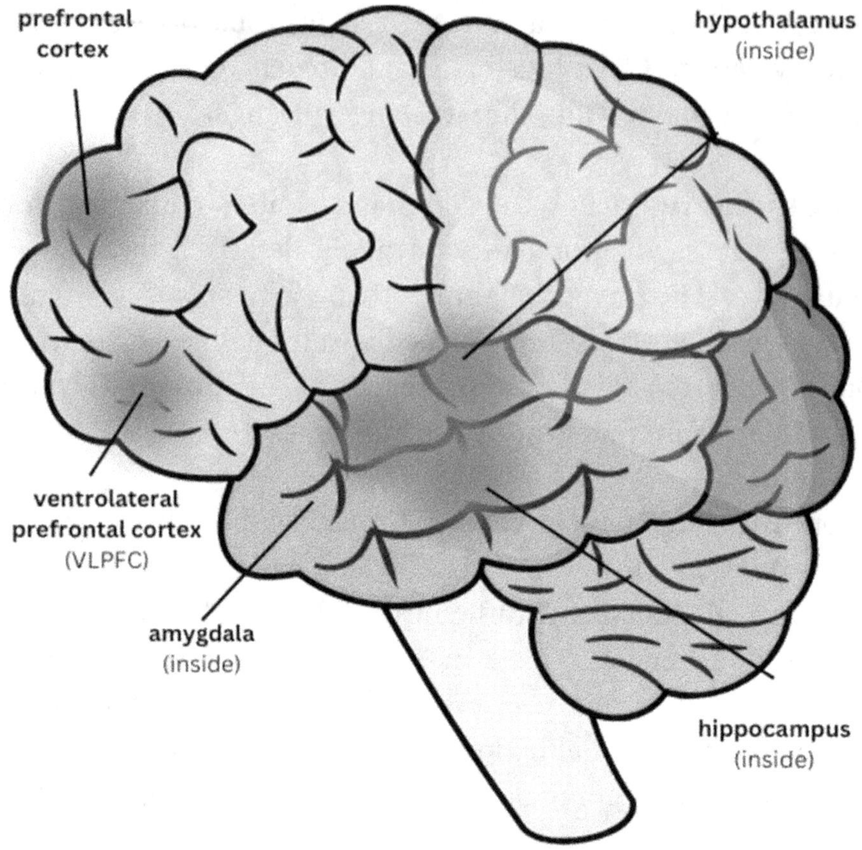

Disclaimer: *The brain anatomy image provided is for reference purposes only. It's a simplified representation and doesn't include all anatomical details or variations. Please refer to a medical practitioner or reliable educational sites for precise and comprehensive medical information.*

Anxiety is an internal distraction. It usually comes as lightning-fast, unconscious thoughts and emotions that *hijack* your state of mind and focus. The great thing is that the human brain can be effectively trained! The key lies in that part of our brains called the ventrolateral prefrontal cortex (VLPFC). Think of it as a control center that helps you manage your thoughts and behaviors, especially when feeling anxious.

Key Functions of the VLPFC

- **Decision Making**: Helps you make choices, especially when you need to weigh different options.

- **Emotion Regulation**: Helps control your emotions, keeping them in check.
- **Attention and Focus**: Helps you concentrate on tasks and ignore distractions.
- **Inhibitory Control**: Helps you stop yourself from doing something impulsive.

Example: Imagine you're at a social gathering and feeling anxious about meeting new people. Your VLPFC helps you decide to introduce yourself instead of retreating to a corner (*decision-making*), calm your nerves by reminding yourself that it's okay to feel nervous (*emotion regulation*), focus on the conversation at hand rather than worrying about what others think (*attention and focus*), and resist the urge to leave early (*inhibitory control*).

So, **how do you train your VLPFC?** Mindfulness is the key. Remember, anxiety is an internal distraction that *hijacks* your state of mind and focus. So when intrusive anxious thoughts arise, it's important to have the skill to gently redirect your attention to the present moment (back to reality). (See Chapter 4: Mindfulness for a deeper dive into cultivating mindfulness, page 50.)

Important: It's important to note that anxiety not only affects the brain, but it can physically change the brain's structure and function over time.[3] If anxiety remains unaddressed, the amygdala (the brain's alarm system and emotion center) may grow larger, making it even more sensitive to perceived threats. Conversely, the prefrontal cortex (responsible for focusing and decision-making) and the hippocampus (involved in emotion regulation and memory) may shrink, weakening their ability to manage stress and regulate emotions effectively. Basically, the longer anxiety is not addressed, the more these changes can become entrenched, making it harder to break the cycle of anxiety and restore normal brain function.

Important: Untreated anxiety can also lead to the development of other conditions, such as insomnia[4], obesity[5,6], chronic pain[7], depression[8,9], heart disease[10,11], and more. Bottom line: the sooner you address anxiety, the better.

What Type of Anxiety Do I Have?

Anxiety is the most common mental health condition, and reports indicate that it affects nearly 30% of US adults at some point throughout their lives.[12] Globally, anxiety affects nearly 300 million people.[13] It also comes in various shapes and sizes. I had Generalized Anxiety Disorder or GAD. Please read below and see which one best describes your current situation. Having an idea of what type of anxiety you have will guide you better moving forward. If you think you might be dealing with any of the types of anxiety mentioned below, please don't hesitate to speak with your doctor.

1. **Generalized Anxiety Disorder (GAD)**: Excessive, uncontrollable worry about everyday things such as health, work, or social interactions. This worry is often out of proportion to the actual situation.

   Symptoms: Restlessness, fatigue, difficulty concentrating, irritability, muscle tension, and sleep disturbances.

2. **Panic Disorder**: Recurrent and unexpected panic attacks, which are sudden periods of intense fear that may include feelings of impending doom.

   Symptoms: Rapid heart rate, sweating, trembling, shortness of breath, feelings of choking, chest pain, nausea, dizziness, and fear of losing control or dying.

3. **Social Anxiety Disorder (SAD, or Social Phobia)**: Intense fear of social situations where one may be judged, embarrassed, or humiliated. SAD has been increasing in recent years.[14] The increasing use of social media, which drastically decreased the need for face-to-face interactions contributed to this. The COVID-19 pandemic also exacerbated social phobia because of the prolonged social isolation we all had to go through.[15]

   Symptoms: Fear of speaking in public, avoiding social gatherings, extreme self-consciousness, and worry about being judged.

4. **Specific Phobias:** Intense, irrational fear of specific objects or situations, such as heights, animals, or flying. The fear is usually out of proportion to the actual danger posed.

   Symptoms: Immediate anxiety response when exposed to the phobic object or situation, avoidance behavior, and sometimes physical symptoms like sweating or trembling.

5. **Agoraphobia**: Fear of being in situations where escape might be difficult or help prove to be unavailable if panic-like symptoms occur.

   Symptoms: Avoidance of certain places, feeling trapped or helpless, and experiencing panic-like symptoms when in feared situations.

6. **Separation Anxiety Disorder**: Excessive fear or anxiety about being separated from attachment figures, such as parents or loved ones. This is more common in children but can also occur in adults.

   Symptoms: Excessive distress when anticipating or experiencing separation, worry about losing attachment figures, refusal to go out due to fear of separation, and physical symptoms like headaches or stomachaches when separation occurs.

7. **Selective Mutism**: Consistent inability to speak in certain social situations where speaking is expected despite speaking in other situations. This is often seen in children.

   Symptoms: Inability to speak in specific settings (e.g., school), speaking normally in comfortable settings (e.g., home), and avoiding speaking-related situations.

8. **Health Anxiety (Hypochondriasis)**: Excessive worry about having a serious illness despite medical reassurance and lack of significant symptoms.

Symptoms: Constantly checking for signs of illness, frequent doctor visits, and avoiding activities due to fear of health problems.

9. **Substance/Medication-Induced Anxiety Disorder**: Anxiety symptoms that are directly caused by substance use, withdrawal, or exposure to medication.
   Symptoms: Intense anxiety or panic attacks, restlessness, difficulty concentrating, and physical symptoms like rapid heart rate or sweating, occurring during or shortly after substance use or withdrawal.

10. **Anxiety Disorder Due to Another Medical Condition**: Significant anxiety symptoms that are the direct result of a medical condition. For example, conditions like hyperthyroidism, heart disease, chronic pain, etc., can cause anxiety symptoms.[16]

   Symptoms: Excessive worry, panic attacks, or other anxiety symptoms directly linked to the medical condition, often alongside symptoms of the underlying medical issue.

A note about Post-Traumatic Stress Disorder (PTSD):
PTSD used to be classified as an anxiety disorder because it involves symptoms like intense fear, panic attacks, and extreme anxiety. However, in 2013, the American Psychiatric Association (APA) re-categorized it in the updated Diagnostic and Statistical Manual of Mental Disorders (DSM-5) under "Trauma- and Stressor-Related Disorders." This is to reflect PTSD's direct connection to traumatic experiences.

A note about Obsessive-Compulsive Disorder (OCD):
Just like PTSD, OCD was re-classified in 2013 in the updated DSM-5 under "Obsessive-Compulsive and Related Disorders." This is to reflect OCD's unique features, which are the presence of obsessions (repeated, persistent, and unwanted thoughts, urges, or images that cause distress or anxiety) and compulsions (repetitive behaviors or mental acts one feels driven to perform in response to an obsession).

Body Dysmorphic Disorder (BDD), often thought of as an anxiety disorder, is also classified under "Obsessive-Compulsive and Related Disorders." This is to highlight BDD's primary characteristics of *obsessive thoughts* about perceived flaws and the *compulsive behaviors* performed to address these thoughts.

Important: Although PTSD, OCD, and BDD are not categorized as an anxiety disorder, anxiety IS a key characteristic of these disorders. As such, the skills you'll learn in this book will greatly benefit you if you suffer from these problems. In particular, you'll learn how to survive or tolerate moments of high stress and anxiety associated with these symptoms (Chapters 6) and how to manage the unhelpful thoughts that characterize these disorders (Chapters 7 and 8).

Worksheet 1: Anxiety Self-Assessment Questionnaire

Still unsure about what type of anxiety you may have? While there isn't a single simple test that can definitively diagnose anxiety disorders, there are screening tools that can help you understand if you might have an anxiety disorder and its severity. One widely used tool is the Generalized Anxiety Disorder 7 (GAD-7).[17] Here's how it works:

For each question below, rate how often you have been bothered by the following problems over the past two weeks. Use the following scale:

0 = Not at all
1 = Several days
2 = More than half the days
3 = Nearly every day

How often have you been bothered by the following problems?	Not at all	Several days	More than half the days	Nearly every day
Feeling nervous, anxious, or on edge	0	1	2	3
Not being able to stop or control worrying	0	1	2	3
Worrying too much about different things	0	1	2	3
Trouble relaxing	0	1	2	3
Being so restless that it is hard to sit still	0	1	2	3
Becoming easily annoyed or irritable	0	1	2	3
Feeling afraid as if something awful might happen	0	1	2	3

Scoring:

0-4: Minimal anxiety

5-9: Mild anxiety

10-14: Moderate anxiety

15-21: Severe anxiety

What to Do Next: Scoring in the 0-4 range indicates you likely have minimal anxiety. It's still a good idea to practice the techniques in this book to prevent its escalation. For scores 5-9 and above, please try the ACT strategies outlined in this book. If at any point you feel overwhelmed, please don't hesitate to reach out to a mental health professional.

Disclaimer: Please note that the GAD-7 is just a screening tool and not a substitute for a professional diagnosis. If you want an accurate assessment, please talk to a healthcare provider who can provide a more comprehensive evaluation and recommend appropriate treatment options.

What's Causing Your Anxiety?

Anxiety can be caused by a variety of factors, often a combination of them. Following is a quick table of the most common causes. Can you pinpoint the reason(s) for your anxiety?

WHAT CAUSES ANXIETY?				
Genetic	Biological	Psychological	Environmental	Lifestyle
Family history of anxiety	Brain chemistry *(Imbalances in neurotransmitters, such as serotonin, dopamine, and norepinephrine, can affect mood regulation and contribute to anxiety.)*	Negative thinking patterns, cognitive distortions, mind traps, etc.	Work and financial stress	Lack of physical activity

WHAT CAUSES ANXIETY?				
Genetic	Biological	Psychological	Environmental	Lifestyle
Genetic predisposition	Hormonal imbalances *(Fluctuations in hormones, particularly during puberty, pregnancy, menopause, or thyroid issues, can influence anxiety levels.)*	Traumatic experiences	Unstable home environment *(e.g., abuse, neglect, etc.)*	Poor diet *(Lack of essential nutrients like magnesium, zinc, and omega-3 fatty acids can contribute to anxiety.)*
	Chronic illness or medical conditions	Stressful life events *(e.g., loss, divorce, illness, injury, conflict, etc.)*	Social environment *(e.g., difficult relationships, social isolation, academic pressure, tech overload, etc.)*	Substance abuse
		Changing values *(Shifting values or living an inauthentic life can lead to internal conflict, identity crisis, negative self-judgment, etc.)*	Urban living *(Noise pollution, overcrowding, and fast-paced living can increase stress and anxiety.)*	Excessive caffeine or alcohol intake
				Sleep deprivation, excessive caffeine or alcohol intake

STRESS

Many of the causes of anxiety listed above highlight stress as a significant underlying factor. However, it's essential to understand that experiencing stress doesn't necessarily equate to having an anxiety disorder.

Stress is your body's natural response to any demand or challenge. It can be caused by everyday pressures such as work, school, relationships, or major life changes. Stress triggers a "fight or flight" response, releasing hormones like adrenaline and cortisol, which prepare your body to deal with the challenge. Also, stress is caused by circumstance, and when the "cause" is addressed or has passed, stress ends as well.

Anxiety, on the other hand, is an ongoing feeling of worry, nervousness, or unease about something with an uncertain outcome. Now, occasional anxiety is a natural reaction to stress. However, when anxiety becomes excessive, prolonged, and interferes with daily life, it can develop into an anxiety disorder. At this stage, anxiety is continuous, regardless of circumstances.

So, stress is not the same as an anxiety disorder. However, when stress is constant and unrelenting, your body stays in a heightened state of alert. Over time, this can exhaust your body and mind, leading to anxiety symptoms.

We live in very stressful times, so it's unsurprising to be unaware of how stressed you are, which is unhealthy. In fact, many people sort of "slide" into an anxiety disorder because they're NOT fully aware of just how much stress they're carrying! So, even if you did the Anxiety Self-Assessment Questionnaire on page 18 and got a good score, please still do the following exercise.

Worksheet 2: Perceived Stress Scale (PSS)

The Perceived Stress Scale (PSS) is a psychological tool that assesses how various situations affect our emotions and perceived stress.[18] Following is an adapted version of the PSS for anxiety.

For each question below, rate your feelings and thoughts during the <u>last month</u> using the following scale:

0 = Never
1 = Almost Never
2 = Sometimes
3 = Fairly Often
4 = Very Often

1. In the last month, how often have you been upset because of something that happened unexpectedly?
   [ ] Never
   [ ] Almost Never
   [ ] Sometimes
   [ ] Fairly Often
   [ ] Very Often

2. In the last month, how often have you felt you could not control the important things in your life?
   [ ] Never
   [ ] Almost Never
   [ ] Sometimes
   [ ] Fairly Often
   [ ] Very Often

3. In the last month, how often have you felt nervous and "stressed"?
   [ ] Never
   [ ] Almost Never
   [ ] Sometimes
   [ ] Fairly Often

[ ] Very Often

4. In the last month, how often have you felt confident about your ability to handle your personal problems?
   [ ] Never
   [ ] Almost Never
   [ ] Sometimes
   [ ] Fairly Often
   [ ] Very Often

5. In the last month, how often have you felt that things were going your way?
   [ ] Never
   [ ] Almost Never
   [ ] Sometimes
   [ ] Fairly Often
   [ ] Very Often

6. In the last month, how often have you found that you could not cope with everything you had to do?
   [ ] Never
   [ ] Almost Never
   [ ] Sometimes
   [ ] Fairly Often
   [ ] Very Often

7. In the last month, how often have you been able to control irritations in your life?
   [ ] Never
   [ ] Almost Never
   [ ] Sometimes
   [ ] Fairly Often
   [ ] Very Often

8. In the last month, how often have you felt that you were on top of things?
   [ ] Never
   [ ] Almost Never

[ ] Sometimes
[ ] Fairly Often
[ ] Very Often

9. In the last month, how often have you been angered because of things outside your control?
   [ ] Never
   [ ] Almost Never
   [ ] Sometimes
   [ ] Fairly Often
   [ ] Very Often

10. In the last month, how often have you felt difficulties were piling up so high that you could not overcome them?
   [ ] Never
   [ ] Almost Never
   [ ] Sometimes
   [ ] Fairly Often
   [ ] Very Often

Scoring:

Questions 4, 5, 7, and 8 are negative questions. That is, they are phrased so that a lower frequency of these experiences indicates higher stress levels. When scoring these questions, you will need to reverse their scores. For example, if you rated yourself a 4 (Very Often) on these questions, it should be scored as a 0; if you rated yourself a 0 (Never), it should be scored as a 4. For the rest of the questions, normal scoring applies.

Tally your score for all 10 questions. Typically, scores are interpreted as follows:

0-13: Low stress
14-26: Moderate stress
27-40: High stress

Disclaimer: Please note that the PSS is just a screening tool, not a professional diagnosis substitute. If you want an accurate assessment, please talk to a healthcare provider who can comprehensively evaluate your stress levels.

Anxiety in Women

Research shows that women are more likely than men to experience anxiety disorders [19,20,21] due to the following unique aspects:

"M" is for Multitasking

Women often juggle multiple roles, such as work, caregiving, and household responsibilities, which can contribute to higher stress and anxiety levels. (Somehow, we have equated the word "woman" to "multi-tasking!") In addition, external pressures and expectations around appearance, behavior, and success can add to anxiety.

"M" is for Menopause

Menopause marks the end of a woman's reproductive years, typically occurring between ages 45 and 55. This transition involves SIGNIFICANT hormonal changes, particularly a decrease in estrogen and progesterone, which can affect mental health.[22,23]

In addition to hormonal changes, there are also physical symptoms such as hot flashes, night sweats, and sleep disturbances. And let's not forget the psychological impact, too. The transition to menopause can bring about concerns related to aging, body image, and changes in identity, which can exacerbate anxiety.

Anxiety in Men

While anxiety disorders are more commonly diagnosed in women, men also experience significant levels of anxiety. It's just that men are less likely to seek help due to societal expectations and the stigma surrounding mental health.[24,25]

Many years ago, I was watching an episode of Oprah. I don't remember what the topic was exactly and who the male guests were. However, at one point, one of them said something like, "It's just the pressure, the pressure of knowing that it's all up to you to provide. And it's not like you can just call your buddies and vent."

After that episode, I looked at my dad a bit differently. I realized that I just never truly considered and appreciated the fact that he was the sole breadwinner in our home, and I KNEW there were times when money was tight. (By the way, my mom's an amazing homemaker; she and Dad have a great relationship. Still, I can't help but sometimes wonder what my Dad felt during those times.)

In addition to the stigma that discourages men from expressing vulnerability or seeking mental health support, they usually don't even recognize anxiety symptoms! Men are more likely to attribute mental health symptoms to physical health issues instead.

Worksheet 3: Specific Anxiety Triggers

Now that you have a clearer understanding of anxiety and its potential causes, it's important to identify your *specific triggers*. Knowing what (or who) sets off your anxiety will help you tailor the ACT skills you'll learn in the succeeding chapters to your unique needs and experiences. For now, just focus on this exercise to help you determine what sets off or triggers your anxiety.

Step 1. Daily Reflection. For TWO WEEKS, take a few minutes each day to reflect on moments when you felt anxious. Don't overthink, analyze, or evaluate anything yet. Just record the event as requested below. (If you need more space, please grab a few sheets of paper or use a notebook or journal.)

Situation: Describe what was happening when you felt anxious.
Example: I was window shopping for some summer clothes.

Location: Where were you?
Example: At the mall.

People Involved: Who were you with?
Example: I was alone.

Thoughts: What were you thinking?

Example: I realized that it was usually with my mom whenever I went window shopping. I was also shocked to realize that I didn't have to stop for food at her favorite place because she was no longer here.

Feelings: Describe your emotions.

Example: I felt loss, grief, sadness, loneliness.

Physical Reactions: Note any physical symptoms.

Example: heart racing, sweating, fast breathing

Step 2. Identify Patterns. After two weeks, look back at your daily reflections to see if common situations, thoughts, or people are associated with your anxiety.

Example: My anxiety seems to be triggered by thoughts of my mother, who passed away recently.

Step 3. Dissect the Trigger. Once you identify a potential trigger, break it down into specific elements to understand why it causes anxiety.

What's the trigger?
Example: Thoughts about my mother.

Why do you think it's triggering anxiety?
Example: I suddenly feel completely alone and lost in this world, like I lost my anchor. I think I also lost part of my sense of purpose because, for a long time, I was my mother's caregiver.

Step 4. Record Your Reactions. Note your physical, emotional, and behavioral reactions to the trigger. (This helps recognize the full impact of the trigger.)

Physical Reaction	Emotional Reaction	Behavioral Reaction
Example: My heart races, and I start sweating.	*Example: I start to feel lost and scared.*	*Example: I avoid eye contact and try to leave the situation or area. "Get out of here" is what I want to do.*

It's possible to have more than just one anxiety trigger, so do this exercise as long and as often as you need. As you go through the following chapters and learn various ACT skills and coping techniques, keep track of new triggers you identify. This ongoing awareness will help you apply what you learn more effectively, ensuring that you address all the factors contributing to your anxiety.

Important: It's extremely helpful to determine the cause of your anxiety. However, note that it's NOT necessary to know its cause to find relief. You can still use all of the techniques in this book to manage and reduce your anxiety because they focus on symptom management and building mental and emotional flexibility. These strategies can help you achieve significant anxiety relief and improve your quality of life, regardless of whether you know the exact cause of your anxiety or not.

How Anxiety Hurts You

Unaddressed anxiety can have a wide range of negative effects in life. I know because I think I've experienced pretty much most of the things you'll read below. Are you experiencing any of the following?

Emotional Health

- **Increased irritability.** Anxiety is often associated with internal turmoil and feelings of inadequacy, but did you know that it can manifest as anger?[26,27] Anxiety often makes you more prone to irritability and mood swings, and small issues may trigger disproportionate emotional responses. Impact: This can strain your relationships with family, friends, and coworkers, creating a cycle of frustration and misunderstanding.

- **Persistent worry and fear.** Untreated anxiety can lead to feelings of being overwhelmed and a persistent sense of dread. Impact: You might find it difficult to enjoy life, even its simplest pleasures.

- **Low self-esteem.** Anxiety can make you doubt your abilities and worth, leading to negative self-perception and reduced confidence. Impact: This can hinder your personal and professional growth and discourage you from pursuing new opportunities.

- **Emotional exhaustion.** Chronic anxiety can drain you emotionally, leading to feelings of exhaustion and burnout. Impact: This can reduce your ability to cope with daily stresses and responsibilities, further exacerbating anxiety symptoms.

- **Feelings of hopelessness.** Persistent anxiety can lead to feelings of hopelessness and helplessness because you feel trapped in your anxious thoughts and unable to find relief. Impact: This can increase your risk of depression and decrease your motivation to seek help or make positive changes.

- **Social withdrawal.** Anxiety can make social interactions feel overwhelming, leading individuals to withdraw from social activities and isolate themselves. Impact: Social isolation can lead to loneliness, further deteriorating emotional health and reducing support networks.

- **Difficulty experiencing pleasure.** Unaddressed anxiety may make it hard to enjoy activities you once found pleasurable due to constant worry and tension. Impact: This can reduce overall life satisfaction and contribute to *anhedonia*, a core symptom of depression.

Physical Health

- **Chronic health problems.** Persistent anxiety can contribute to the development or worsening of chronic health conditions such as heart disease, hypertension, and gastrointestinal issues.

- **Weakened immune system.** Ongoing anxiety can weaken the immune system, making the body more susceptible to infections and illnesses.

- **Sleep disturbances.** Anxiety often leads to difficulty falling asleep or staying asleep, resulting in poor sleep quality and chronic fatigue.

- **Muscle tension and pain.** Constant anxiety can cause muscle tension, leading to headaches, back pain, and other musculoskeletal issues.

Mental Health

- **Depression.** Unaddressed anxiety can lead to or exacerbate depression, creating a cycle of worsening mental health.

- **Substance abuse.** Some individuals may turn to alcohol, drugs, or other substances to cope with anxiety, which can lead to substance abuse and addiction.

- **Cognitive impairment.** Chronic anxiety can affect concentration, memory, and decision-making abilities, impacting daily tasks and overall cognitive function.

Daily Functioning

- **Work performance.** Anxiety can impair job performance by causing difficulties in concentration, decision-making, and maintaining productivity. It may also lead to increased absenteeism.

- **Academic challenges.** For students, anxiety can impact academic performance by affecting concentration, test performance, and participation in school activities.

Long-Term Consequences

- **Decreased quality of life.** Chronic anxiety can significantly diminish one's overall quality of life, limiting opportunities and experiences.

- **Ruined relationships.** Anxiety can make you physically and emotionally absent. Missing out on important events, neglecting responsibilities, or being unable to provide the support and presence important people in your life need can strain relationships to the point of breaking.

- **Development of comorbid conditions.** Untreated anxiety can lead to the development of other mental health conditions, such as depression, obsessive-compulsive disorder (OCD) or post-traumatic stress disorder (PTSD).

- **Increased risk of self-harm.** Severe, untreated anxiety can increase the risk of self-harm and suicidal thoughts and behaviors, particularly if it coexists with depression.

I know that this may all seem daunting. However, I can tell you from experience that inaction is the last thing you should do. Relief IS possible. Here's my tip: just take this ACT journey with me, *one page at a time*.

Start learning about anxiety relief on the next page...

Chapter 2: What is Acceptance and Commitment Therapy?

"Sometimes the smallest step in the right direction ends up being the biggest step of your life. Tiptoe if you must, but take the step." – Naeem Callaway

Acceptance and Commitment Therapy (ACT) was developed in the 1980s by prominent psychologist Steven C. Hayes[28], and his personal and professional experiences influenced it.

You see, long before he became a psychologist, Hayes struggled with panic disorder. So, his personal experience with anxiety and panic attacks played a significant role in shaping his approach to therapy. Professionally, Hayes and his colleagues would be working with people struggling with psychological problems such as anxiety and depression. And, well, he just thought that there's got to be a better way to help people struggling with these issues, so ACT was born.

As with many forms of psychotherapy, ACT is influenced by other therapies. It draws from:

- **Behaviorism** emphasizes the influence of our environment and learning experiences on our behavior.

  For example, imagine you touched a hot stove as a child and got burned. Because of that painful experience, you learned to avoid touching hot stoves. This is behaviorism in action: your behavior (avoiding hot stoves) is shaped by your past experience (getting burned).

- **Relational Frame Theory (RFT)** is about how our minds connect words, thoughts, and experiences in ways that can sometimes cause stress or anxiety.

For example, suppose that you had to make a school project presentation as a teen. You were nervous, so you stuttered and said something incorrect. Your classmates laughed, and you were made fun of for weeks. After that, whenever you hear the word "presentation," you feel nervous and anxious. This happens because your brain has linked the word "presentation" with the memory of failing and the feelings of stress from that experience.

- **Cognitive Behavioral Therapy (CBT) and Behavioral Therapy** focus on modifying maladaptive or unhelpful behavior.

  For example, suppose you experience tremendous stress before work deadlines. In CBT, you might work on changing your thoughts from "I'll NEVER finish on time!" to "I've prepared enough. This should help to finish on time." Meanwhile, in Behavioral Therapy, you might practice relaxation techniques, like deep breathing or progressive muscle relaxation, to reduce anxiety before the looming deadline.

In addition to the above influences, ACT incorporates acceptance- and mindfulness-based strategies and values-based living to help develop *psychological flexibility*.

Psychological flexibility is about resilience or your "bounce-back ability." It's your capability to come back from setbacks, adjust to changing circumstances, and thrive despite your anxiety.

You see, ACT acknowledges that life is full of ups and downs. The secret is enjoying the ups and developing the flexibility and resilience to navigate the downs. One thing that's very important to realize is that when you work on yourself, your mental and emotional resilience improves! This means that something that triggers your anxiety today might not have the same impact on you tomorrow. Now, isn't that thought a relief in itself?

So, how do you develop psychological flexibility?

ACT: Original Hexaflex Model

Psychological flexibility can be developed by practicing these skills: *Acceptance, Mindfulness, Cognitive Defusion, Self as Context, Values Clarification,* and *Committed Action.*

ACT: My Expanded Model

Before discussing the six core principles of ACT, I'd like to include a skill I learned in DBT: **Willingness**.

When I started my healing journey, I found myself... *resisting*. I think that after years of ignoring my anxiety, something inside me was avoiding dealing with it head-on.

Call it fear, call it ignorance, call it bullheadedness... whatever it was, I needed to get over it. Why? Because whatever I was doing up to that point was clearly NOT working. (Otherwise, I wouldn't have ended up experiencing anxiety-induced burnout and a breakdown.)

As I talked to more people, I realized many face the same issue. Oh, we WANT to get better, but for many of us, there's some reluctance we need to overcome first. Otherwise, no amount of information and skills training will be effective. So, I'd like to expand on the ACT framework to this:

Disclaimer: Please note that this expansion is based on my personal experiences and the insights I've gained from others who have shared similar journeys. While I believe this additional focus on Willingness is vital, it's not part of the original ACT framework. Also, I want to clarify that I'm not a licensed mental health professional; the information I share is meant to complement, not replace, professional advice or treatment.

Note: ACT core principles are interconnected, working together to promote psychological flexibility. Although I highly encourage you to go over them in the order presented in this book, you don't necessarily have to do them in sequence. Depending on what feels most relevant to your journey, you can focus on one principle more than others at different times. The key is to integrate these principles into your life in a natural and supportive way.

Gentle reminder: The best way to benefit from the ACT skills in this book is to continuously practice the exercises *before* you need them. Doing so will make you more prepared to apply them whenever anxiety arises.

Chapter 3: Willingness

"Willingness is the key to transformation. It's the first step towards the life you desire." — Unknown

Willingness is openness to experience thoughts and emotions without avoidance. It's a commitment to engage with life as it is, even when it involves doubt, discomfort, or fear. Resistance or unwillingness can be due to various reasons, including:

- **Emotional pain.** Healing often requires facing painful emotions or experiences. This can lead to resistance, especially if you prefer to stay in your comfort zone rather than confront difficult feelings. <u>Mindset change</u>: Discomfort is a natural part of healing. No bruise ever got better without going through some form of pain.

- **Fear of change.** Change can be intimidating, and you may fear the unknown that comes with confronting your anxiety. <u>Mindset change</u>: If you don't take the step to change, you'll stay exactly where you are right now.

- **Fear of vulnerability.** No one likes feeling vulnerable. This was my personal roadblock. I HATED showing any sign of weakness because then people might discover that I was struggling inside. But then I told myself, "Well, you ARE struggling, Ava. How much more are you willing to punish yourself?" <u>Mindset change</u>: Sometimes, we need to be weak and vulnerable to be strong.

- **Doubt in effectiveness.** You may question whether what you learn in this book will help you or whether it's worth your time and effort. <u>Mindset change</u>: Everyone's path to healing is unique, and you won't know what works for you... until you try something that might work for you.

- **Perceived stigma.** There's STILL stigma around prioritizing one's self and seeking help. <u>Mindset change</u>: Seeking help for your anxiety is a sign of strength, not weakness. It's okay to prioritize your mental health and well-being, just as you would for any physical ailment.

- **Unrealistic expectations.** You might expect quick fixes or immediate results. You might even tell yourself, "Well, if I don't feel anything different in the next day or so, this is not for me." Pre-setting unrealistic results is a clear sign of unwillingness. It means you're not 100% open to whatever may happen in your journey. <u>Mindset change</u>: There's no time limit or "deadline" for managing and overcoming anxiety. Think of yourself as a wonderful flowering plant. Just nourish it. It will bloom when it's ready.

- **Fear of hope.** When it comes to mental health healing, I believe most of us are afraid to hope because hope can feel like a double-edged sword. Hoping means you risk feeling disappointed. To quote Finnick Odair, one of my favorite characters in the film The Hunger Games, "It takes ten times as long to put yourself back together as it does to fall apart."

  However, I've learned that giving in to "fear of hope" means we become unwilling to take risks. And risk is the only way to potentially achieve change. <u>Mindset change</u>: Don't be afraid of hope; rather, be wearier of staying in place. Don't underestimate yourself. Better days are possible, but only if you're willing to pursue them.

So, willingness is crucial to healing, but HOW do you cultivate it? What do you do? Following are various exercises specifically crafted to help you embrace a greater sense of willingness in your journey.

Worksheet 4: Willing Hands

Willing Hands is a perfect example of the mind-body connection in action. By focusing on your hands, you can influence your mind to be more open and willing.

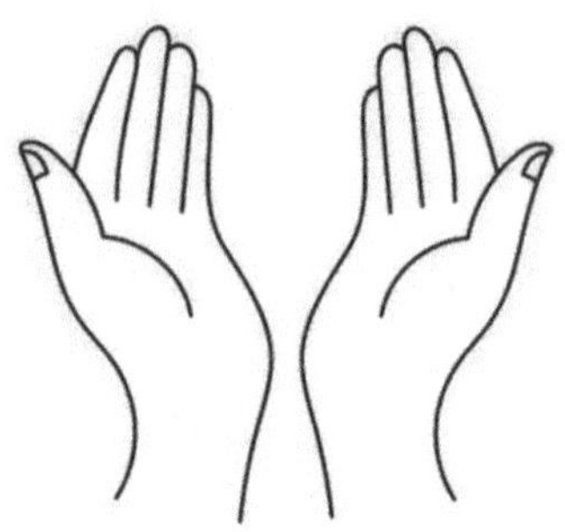

Step 1. Find a comfortable position. Sit or stand in a quiet place where you won't be disturbed. Ensure your back is straight and your feet are flat on the ground.

Step 2. Relax your hands on your thighs with palms facing upward. Let your fingers naturally curl in a relaxed position.

Step 3. Take a few deep breaths, inhaling through your nose and exhaling through your mouth.

Step 4. On your next inhale, **slowly close your hands.** Don't make a tight fist. Just gently close them. As you exhale, **slowly open your hands and palms** and relax your fingers. **Tip**: Include a positive, willing-focused thought as you open your hands. For example, you can say, "I'm open to new," "I'm willing," "I'm ready for change," or "I'm willing to discover [your name] 2.0."

Step 5. If you're still feeling any resistance, do step 4 above a few more times until you feel tension or resistance fade.

Worksheet 5: Vulnerability

As mentioned, fear of vulnerability is one of the main reasons why we might be unwilling to do anything new or different. This exercise aims to help you practice vulnerability by gradually opening up about your feelings, thoughts, and experiences in a safe and controlled manner.

Step 1. Reflect on what vulnerability means to you. Consider why you might be afraid or don't want to feel vulnerable by completing the sentence below. (Write as many reasons you can think of.)

I don't like feeling vulnerable because:

Example: I don't want others to see my struggles and judge me.

Step 2. Write a brief paragraph about how practicing vulnerability might help you.

Example: Maybe if I can be vulnerable, I can RELAX in my relationships because I'm not always "on guard."

Step 3. Identify your "safe people." Name a few trusted individuals with whom you feel comfortable sharing your feelings. These could be close friends, family members, or a therapist.

Example: Rose. I trust my wife more than anyone. Also, I know she's been worried about me lately. Next to her would be Martin, my best friend since grade school. Although it's so tough to "share" with guys, I trust Martin.

Step 4. Share minor vulnerabilities. There's no need to rush this process and have a "big reveal" (unless that's what you want). So start by sharing something small but personal with one of your trusted individuals. This could be a minor worry or a recent disappointment.

Example: Babe, I get really anxious in the morning during breakfast; just the RUSH of it all. I feel overwhelmed, and sort of can't think straight. I worry about whether I'm eating the right thing, if I'll have enough time, if I'll be late for work... it's a whirlwind of thoughts that makes starting my day really tough.

Important: It's a BIG step on your part to decide to share something. However, if the other person has no clue about your anxiety, please be patient and don't feel bad if they don't react the way you want them to. The most important thing here is your decision to share something and allow yourself to be vulnerable.

At the same time, be prepared for questions. If the person to which you opened up asks you how they can help, let them know.

What help do you need?
Example: I'd appreciate a bit more routine to our mornings so I don't start the day overwhelmed.

On the other hand, if you just want to share, that's okay too. You can say, "I'm just sharing for now so you understand how I feel and what's happening with me. I'm not ready yet to dive into this topic further. Please be patient."

Step 5. Gradually share more significant experiences. As you become more comfortable, gradually share more significant thoughts and feelings. This could involve discussing deeper fears, past experiences, or ongoing struggles.

Step 6. Be kind to yourself. Practice self-compassion, especially if you feel exposed or uncomfortable after being vulnerable. It would help if you have a self-compassionate statement you can read to yourself regularly. Here are a few examples:
   [ ] It's good to share my feelings.
   [ ] It's okay to feel vulnerable. I'm taking steps to improve my well-being.
   [ ] Vulnerability is a strength, not a weakness.
   [ ] It's normal to feel anxious sometimes. I'm allowed to experience my thoughts and emotions without judgment.

[ ] I'm doing my best, and that's enough. Every step I take is part of my healing journey.

Step 7. Share with a wider circle. Once you're comfortable with your trusted individuals, consider expanding your circle of vulnerability. This might include sharing in support groups, at work, or in social settings when appropriate.

Step 8. Reflect and adjust. Continuously reflect on your experiences with vulnerability. Note what works well and what doesn't. Adjust your approach as needed. **Tip**: Keep a vulnerability journal where you document your journey, progress, and insights.

Step 9. Acknowledge your growth! Celebrate your efforts and progress in practicing vulnerability. Acknowledge the courage it takes to open up and the positive changes you've experienced.

Worksheet 6: Switching the Struggle OFF

An unwilling person is a struggling person. For example, it might be that something inside you doubts the efficacy of ACT to give you anxiety relief. This doubt is causing your unwillingness to learn the skills in this book, or it might make you do the activities here half-heartedly.

This exercise aims to help you recognize and reduce any internal resistance to engaging with the skills presented in this book. By "switching off the struggle," you can open yourself to learning and applying ACT effectively.

Step 1. Identify your doubts. Take a moment to reflect on any doubts or concerns you have about using ACT to help with your anxiety. Write down any thoughts that come to mind.

Your Doubts:

Examples:
I don't think this will work for me.
I've tried other things before, and they didn't help, so why would this one?
This may be too complicated for me.

Step 2. Acknowledge your feelings. Recognize that it's okay to feel uncertain or skeptical. Write down how these doubts make you feel physically and emotionally.

Your Feelings:

Examples:
I feel unsure.

I feel worried that nothing will help me.

Step 3. What else? Think about what life can be like if you surrender to the process for just a minute.

What else could happen?

Examples:
I could get some relief from my anxiety.
I could finally take that trip I've always wanted but never could due to my anxiety.
I could be happier.

Step 4. Switch off the struggle. Keeping your answers in the previous step in mind, visualize any doubts and resistance as a switch you can turn off. Picture yourself physically flipping the switch down to "OFF." As you do this, take a deep breath and allow the tension of those doubts to fade away. Write down how you feel after "switching off" those thoughts.

After switching off the struggle...

Example: I know my worries are still there but I'm entertaining the potential positive outcomes more now.

Just sharing: I also like imagining my unwillingness as words, sentences, or even a poster inside a room with me. I then imagine flipping the lights in the room to "OFF," getting out of the room, and closing the door. Kind of like leaving my unwillingness behind.

Step 5. Write a commitment statement to yourself, emphasizing your willingness to engage with the skills in this book. Remind yourself why you want to work on your anxiety.

Example:
I commit to embracing the skills outlined in this book to help manage my anxiety. I want to feel more in control of my thoughts and emotions, improve my relationships, and live a fulfilling life. I'm willing to face discomfort and uncertainty to find relief and build a more resilient self. I commit to showing up for myself and taking the steps necessary to create positive change in my life.

Your Commitment Statement:

Chapter 4: Mindfulness

"The greatest gift you can give yourself is a little bit of your own attention." — Anthony J. D'Angelo

Mindfulness is living in NOW, which is often against anxiety. How? An anxious mind often lives in the past or the future.

Myra[1] has suffered from anxiety ever since she can remember, which has made her a very meticulous planner. From a young age, she mapped out every aspect of her life. She kept a calendar filled with reminders, to-do lists, and goals—nearly every minute of her day accounted for.

Despite her efforts, Myra frequently felt overwhelmed. Instead of feeling confident in her plans, she often worries about forgetting to include something important on her lists. This anxiety would lead her to repeatedly check her lists, and even after reassuring herself that she had written everything down, she would begin to fret about whether she had enough time to complete it all.

As each year passed, Myra's anxiety grew, and so did her lists. She would laugh when her sister would say, "Myra, your lists have lists!" but deep inside, she was hurting deeply.

Because of the constant "jokes" about her lists, she started withdrawing socially. She eventually quit her job as a Team Leader in a data processing company (she couldn't handle the stress of being responsible for a project and the anxiety of dealing with people) and took freelance data entry jobs at home. This, of course, shrunk her social circle even more.

---

[1] *Name changed for privacy.*

"At one point, I just noticed that I was sort of "stuck." I wanted to have conversations, but I get anxious just thinking about talking to people. I was lonely, but I didn't want to go out.

When family members visit (and they MUST schedule it with me first!), I would be anxious the minute the visit was set, terrified while they were here, and I couldn't sleep properly for days because I would relive every moment of the visit in my mind. I was stuck between loneliness and the discomfort of any form of connection."

One day, as she sat at her desk scrolling through social media, Myra stumbled upon a quote from the Dalai Lama that goes something like this, "The past is already gone. The future is not yet here. There's only one moment for you to live" and "Man is so anxious about the future that he does not enjoy the present, the result being that he never lives in the present."

"For some reason, those quotes really got to me. In one crystal clear moment, I saw myself as someone never living in the present, and maybe that meant I wasn't really "living" at all."

Myra wondered if she could truly just "live in the moment." Intrigued, she decided to give mindfulness a try. She started with just five minutes each morning. She would wake up, sit in bed, close her eyes, and focus on her breath.

"Believe it or not, my "list habit" helped. I scheduled those five minutes, so in my mind, I had to do them. So, getting started was not a problem, but it felt hard and awkward. So many thoughts flooded my mind. My schedule... did I check that I have what I need for breakfast last night... what if the phone rings? I found it very challenging to quiet my mind and let go of my worries."

Myra realized she needed something to focus on during those five minutes, so she turned to Breath Counting. She would inhale and say "1", exhale and say "2", inhale again and say "3," etc. The goal was to get to 20 mindfully. If she lost count, she had to start all over again at "1". She would do this until her five minutes were up. Gradually, Myra started to notice a shift in her attention.

"At the start, it was about the focus on the counting. But at one point, I began to notice the gentle rhythm of my breath. When I inhaled, I didn't just count anymore; I also felt the cool air enter my nostrils and the warm air leave my mouth as I exhaled. I learned to invite a sense of calm with each inhale, and with each exhale, I tried to let go of any tension I physically felt. I got excited. Is this mindfulness? Am I capable of being "in the moment" now?

Pretty soon, the five minutes turned to 10, which turned to 15 on a thick towel on the flower. The mindfulness turned to yoga, which gave me this intense desire to buy a yoga mat... but not online. For the first time in a very long time, I called my sister to see if she wanted to go out and buy a yoga mat with me. She was shocked and so happy for me. Her reaction made me cry. I didn't know how much I had missed that connection until that moment.

I have a long way to go. I know that. But I have some fragile sense of peace now that I don't think I've ever felt. I still have anxiety. I know that, too. But my mind doesn't rush like a runaway train in the mornings so much anymore. I'm hopeful all this positive change will continue to grow and spread."

Yes, mindfulness is being present, but it's not just about existing in the moment. It's about creating that gateway to *true awareness*. If you notice, Myra started with mindful breath counting, but it took a while for her to be fully aware of HOW she was breathing, to actually feel and experience how air entered and exited her body,

Mindful awareness is a crucial starting point to anxiety relief because you can't accept your anxiety, be compassionate about it, and address it if you haven't first fully recognized its presence—and effects—in your life.

I think of mindfulness as a valuable tool for managing anxiety both in the short term and in the long term.

Short-term. When anxious, you enter "automatic" or "knee-jerk reaction" mode. Something happens (trigger), you get anxious (emotion), and you react (behavior)—all in seconds or minutes. Mindfulness gives you the time, space, and opportunity to *think before you act.*

For example, suppose you have Social Anxiety Disorder (SAD). But, determined to face your fears, you finally agree to join a friend for coffee. You worry that you'll be late, so you arrive early. You sit down, and now you're worried if your friend will even arrive.

Your friend arrives (whew!), but they're not alone. This is NOT what you agreed to, and your anxiety skyrockets. You feel a rush of panic and start feeling cornered and overwhelmed. Your friend and their companion reach your table, but before they can even sit, you stand up, mumble an excuse, grab your things, and rush out of the coffee shop.

Later that night, you torment yourself and drown in a mix of embarrassment and frustration. You realize that your knee-jerk reaction was driven by your intense anxiety, causing you to flee without considering the situation fully. That is where mindfulness helps you in the short term.

When a trigger occurs, mindfulness enables you to take a mental step back and be in the moment (present awareness) so you can assess the situation fully and objectively. This helps prevent you from making knee-jerk reactions that might worsen the situation.

Long-term. At the same time, something amazing happens when you keep practicing mindfulness even when you don't need it. You start developing that *psychological flexibility*. It's like gaining "mental muscle." The more you exercise mindfulness, the better you become at handling moments of stress and anxiety. And that's not just theory; science shows that with *continued practice*, mindfulness:

- **Reduces stress.**[29,30] Mindfulness helps you stop dwelling on worries, like constantly replaying a stressful conversation or fearing what might go wrong in the future. By focusing on the present moment, you train yourself to acknowledge and let go of anxious thoughts faster, reducing the overall feeling of stress.

- **Improves focus.**[31,32] When you struggle with anxiety, your mind can feel scattered, jumping from one worry to another. Practicing mindfulness, specifically Focused-Attention (FA) meditation, trains your mind to concentrate on one task at a time. (See Candle Meditation, page 59.)

For example, suppose you get anxious when talking to people you just met. If you have improved focus, you can fully engage in a conversation with them instead of worrying about saying something "wrong" or overthinking your responses. This allows you to listen actively, respond genuinely, and build connections rather than being trapped in your anxious thoughts.

- **Enhances emotional regulation.**[33,34] Mindfulness allows you to acknowledge and accept your emotions *without judgment*. For example, when you feel anxious before a big presentation, instead of trying to push those feelings away, mindfulness teaches you to recognize that anxious thoughts and feelings are just that—thoughts and feelings. By accepting that you are having them in the moment, you can better manage your reaction to them.

Ready to be more mindful? The following exercise will help you achieve just that.

Worksheet 7: Mindful Breathing for Stress Relief

This exercise is designed to help you manage stress and anxiety using the power of deep breathing and visualization.

Step 1. Sit or lie down in a comfortable position. Ensure your back is straight but not rigid to allow for deep breathing.

Step 2. Gently place one hand on your heart and the other on your belly. This simple gesture creates a sense of warmth and safety in your mind and body. If you feel comfortable, close your eyes to help you focus inward.

Step 3. Inhale slowly and deeply through your nose. Feel your chest and abdomen expand as you fill your lungs with air. Feel your hands ride that gentle up-and-down wave as you inhale slowly and exhale deeply.

Step 4. Pause briefly. Hold your breath for a moment at the top of the inhale. Notice the stillness and fullness in your lungs.

Step 5. Exhale slowly and completely through your mouth. Feel your body release tension with each out-breath. **Tip**: Say "Go" as you exhale, signifying the release of the stress you're experiencing.

Step 6. Repeat the breathing cycle. Continue this breathing pattern: inhale deeply through your nose, hold for a moment, and exhale slowly through your mouth. Repeat for several minutes.

Step 7. Focus on the sensation. As you breathe, focus on the sensation of your hand on your heart. Feel the warmth and gentle pressure. Silently remind yourself that it's okay to feel stressed. Affirm to yourself that you are safe and capable of handling your emotions.

Step 8. Visualize your stress. In your mind, assign a color, shape, or texture to your stress. For example, imagine your stress as a crumpled sheet of red paper. Keep this image in your mind's eye. As you breathe out, visualize this crumpled paper slowly smoothing out and untangling with each exhale. Imagine that this is your stress leaving your body.

Step 9. Practice self-compassion. If negative thoughts or strong emotions arise, acknowledge them without judgment. Use self-compassionate statements such as, "It's okay to feel stressed. I'm here for myself now" or "I'm allowed to take this time to care for myself."

Step 10. Continue this mindful breathing practice for 5-10 minutes or as long as needed. Gradually increase the duration as you become more comfortable with the exercise. When you're ready, gently open your eyes. Take a moment to notice how you feel and reflect on any changes in your stress or anxiety levels.

Worksheet 8: Grounding for Anxiety Release

When we're anxious, it often feels like we're being pulled in different directions. We might be thinking about something that happened (past) or worrying about something that might happen (future). This exercise aims to help you manage anxiety by helping you ground yourself in the present moment (now).

Step 1. Find a quiet place to sit comfortably on a chair without distractions.

Step 2. Set a time for this exercise using a timer, your watch, or your mobile phone. Start with 5-10 minutes and gradually increase the time as you become more comfortable.

Step 3. Ground yourself. Begin by grounding yourself in the present moment. Place your feet flat on the floor and feel the connection with the ground. Take a few deep breaths, inhaling through your nose and exhaling through your mouth.

Step 4. Close your eyes and bring your attention to your body. Start with your feet and slowly move your attention upward, noticing tension or discomfort. As you scan each part of your body, try to release any tension. For example, if you notice tension in your toes, consciously relax them.

Step 5. Focus on your breath. Shift your focus to your breath. Notice the sensation of the air entering your nostrils, filling your lungs, and then leaving your body. Pay attention to the rhythm of your breath without trying to change it. Simply observe it as it is.

Step 6. Count your breaths. To help maintain focus, count each breath. Inhale and mentally count "one," exhale and count "two," and continue up to ten. Then start over at one. If your mind wanders, gently bring your attention back to your breath and start counting again.

Step 7. Acknowledge and release thoughts. It's normal for thoughts to arise. When they do, simply acknowledge them without judgment. For example, when a thought arises, imagine it as a stress balloon, and you're holding its string in your hand. When you exhale, imagine releasing your hold on the string. The balloon gently flies away, carrying your worries with it.

Step 8. If it helps, you can **anchor your attention using a calming phrase or mantra.** For example, silently repeat "I am calm" or "This too shall pass" with each breath. Match the mantra to your breathing pattern for added focus.

Step 9. Engage all your senses. To deepen your mindfulness, briefly shift your attention to your senses and notice:

- FIVE things you can see;
- FOUR things you can hear;
- THREE things you can touch or feel;
- TWO things you can smell and
- ONE thing you can taste.

Spend a few moments on each sense, then return your focus to your breath.

Step 10. Practice self-compassion. Be kind to yourself throughout this exercise. If you find it difficult to stay focused or if your anxiety persists, remind yourself that it's okay. Mindfulness is a practice, and it's normal to have challenges. Silently offer yourself phrases of self-compassion, such as "May I be kind to myself," "It's okay to feel this way," or "I will be patient with myself."

Step 11. Gradually end your practice. Take a few deep breaths when your timer goes off or you feel ready to end the exercise. Slowly bring your awareness back to your surroundings. Open your eyes and take a moment to notice how you feel.

Worksheet 9: Candle Meditation

This Focused-Attention exercise is a powerful technique that can help alleviate anxiety by training your mind to concentrate on a single focus point. This practice helps reduce the scattered, overwhelming thoughts that often accompany anxiety, promoting a sense of calm and control.

Step 1. Select a candle that you find pleasant. It can be scented or unscented. Place it in a safe, stable holder.

Step 2. Choose a quiet, comfortable place where you won't be disturbed. Dim the lights to create a calming atmosphere.

Step 3. Set the candle at eye level, about two feet before you. Sit in a comfortable position, either on a chair or on the floor with a cushion.

Step 4. Light the candle and take a moment to get settled in your position. Take a few deep breaths to relax your body and mind.

Step 5. Gently direct your gaze to the flame of the candle. Observe the flame's colors, shapes, and movements without straining your eyes.

Step 6. Start deep breathing. Begin to take slow, deep breaths. Inhale through your nose for a count of four, hold for a count of four, and exhale through your mouth for a count of four. Continue this square breathing pattern throughout the meditation.

Step 7. Observe your thoughts. As you focus on the flame, you may notice thoughts arising in your mind. Simply observe these thoughts without judgment and gently bring your attention to the candle flame.

Step 8. Engage your senses. Notice any scents from the candle if it is scented. Feel the warmth of the flame if you hold your hand near it (but not too close to avoid burns).

Step 9. Anchor yourself in the present. If your mind wanders, gently guide it back to the present moment by focusing on the flame and your breath.

Remind yourself that it's normal for the mind to wander and that the practice is in gently returning to the focus point.

Step 10. Maintain your focus. Continue observing the flame and maintaining your breathing pattern for 5-10 minutes. As you become more comfortable with the practice, you can gradually increase the duration to 15 minutes or longer.

Step 11. Slowly close your focused meditation. When you're ready to end the meditation, slowly bring your attention away from the flame. Take a few deep breaths, close your eyes, and bring your focus inward. Reflect on how you feel after the meditation and notice any changes in your body or mind.

Worksheet 10: Mindful Walking

Mindful walking is a simple yet powerful practice combining mindfulness' benefits with physical activity. By focusing on the present moment as you walk, you ground yourself to "now," providing a break from anxious thoughts.

Step 1. Choose a peaceful location. Find a quiet, safe place where you can walk without interruptions. This could be a park, a quiet street, a community garden, or even your backyard.

Step 2. Stand still and breathe deeply. Before you start walking, take a moment to stand still. Take a few deep breaths. Inhale through your nose, letting your abdomen expand, and exhale through your mouth, releasing any tension.

Step 3. Set an intention. Set a positive intention for your walk. It could be to clear your mind, connect with nature, or simply enjoy the movement.

Step 4. Start walking at a slow and steady pace. Pay attention to the sensation of your feet touching the ground. Do your feet land flat on the ground or roll from heel to toe? Notice the surface texture beneath your feet and how it feels with each step.

Step 5. Focus on your breath. As you walk, bring your attention to your breath. Notice the rhythm of your inhales and exhales. Try to synchronize your steps with your breathing. For example, inhale for two steps and exhale for two steps.

Step 6. Engage your senses. Become aware of your surroundings. Notice the sights, sounds, smells, and even the feel of the air on your skin. This sensory engagement helps anchor you in the present moment.

Step 7. Observe your body. Pay attention to how your body moves. Notice the sensation of your muscles working, your arms swing, and your spine's position. Be mindful of any areas of tension.

Step 8. Visualize your anxiety. If you notice anxious thoughts arising, visualize them as a tangible object in your environment. For instance, imagine your anxiety as a branch or leaf on a tree along your path. As you continue walking and pass the tree, focus on the feeling that you are literally leaving your anxiety behind, moving further away from it with each step.

Step 9. Practice self-compassion. If you find your mind wandering or become distracted, gently bring your attention back to your walking. Use self-compassionate statements like, "It's okay to get distracted. I'll just gently bring my focus back."

Step 10. Conclude your walk with gratitude. After your walk, take a moment to give thanks for the experience. Appreciate the time you dedicated to your well-being and the calmness you've cultivated. Reflect on the sensations you felt, the sights you saw, the images or scenes you've encountered, etc. This gratitude practice can enhance the positive effects of your mindful walk, leaving you with a greater sense of peace and fulfillment.

Worksheet 11: NeuroAffective Touching

NeuroAffective Touching (NAT) is a therapeutic technique that combines mindfulness with gentle physical touch to help alleviate anxiety. By engaging the mind and body, NAT can promote safety, reduce stress, and bring calmness.

Step 1. Find a quiet, comfortable space. Sit or lie down in a place where you won't be disturbed. Ensure your environment is calm and peaceful.

Step 2. Take a few deep breaths to center yourself. Close your eyes if you feel comfortable, and bring your awareness to your body.

Step 3. Choose a focus area. Select an area of your body where you feel tension or discomfort. Common areas include the chest, abdomen, or shoulders.

Step 4. Apply gentle touch. Place your hand gently on the chosen area. Use a light, comforting touch as if you were reassuring a loved one.

Step 5. Focus on the sensation. Direct your attention to the feeling of your hand on your body. Notice its warmth, pressure, and any other physical sensations.

Step 6. Visualize calming energy. The human body is made of energy.[35] As such, imagine a warm, soothing light emanating from your hand, calming that part of your body, feeling stress, anxiety, tension, or discomfort. Visualize this light, spreading warmth and goodwill through your body.

Step 7. Breathe mindfully. Inhale slowly through your nose, feeling your chest or abdomen rise under your hand. Exhale gently through your mouth, noticing the release of tension.

Step 8. Acknowledge your emotions. If strong emotions arise, acknowledge them without judgment. Allow yourself to feel and process these emotions as part of the healing process.

Step 9. Switch focus areas. If you feel the need, move your hand to another area of your body that requires attention. Repeat the process of gentle touch and mindful breathing for each body part that needs it.

Step 10. Gradually end the session. When you feel ready, slowly bring your awareness back to the room. Open your eyes, gently move your hand away, and take a few deep breaths.

Chapter 5: Acceptance

"Acceptance doesn't mean resignation; it means understanding that something is what it is and that there's got to be a way through it." — Michael J. Fox

Acceptance means actively embracing your thoughts, feelings, and experiences without trying to deny, avoid, change, or judge them. It involves opening up to the reality of your inner experiences and allowing them to exist AS IS, even when they are uncomfortable or painful.

I know that it's hard to accept anxiety. For the longest time, I truly didn't want to accept it. I thought that to accept anxiety meant I was "weak," that anxiety won over me somehow, and that by accepting it, I had sealed my faith, and so all hope was gone. I was so wrong! I learned that the secret was NOT to focus on anxiety itself but to relearn what "acceptance" truly means.

Acceptance is NOT being "okay" with anxiety. You are just acknowledging the fact that it currently exists in your life.

Acceptance is NOT surrendering, giving up, or giving in to anxiety. You cannot accept something in the future. So, accepting anxiety means accepting its presence in your life now. It doesn't mean you don't want to get relief from it and change your circumstances moving forward.

Acceptance is NOT about downplaying anxiety's impact. Acceptance only acknowledges. It doesn't under- or overestimate, or under- or overvalue anything.

Acceptance is NOT a sign of weakness. Acceptance builds resilience. When you accept your anxiety, you also accept your amazing capacity to manage it. This builds inner strength and resilience, empowering you to face anxiety with confidence and a sense of control.

Acceptance is NOT shutting yourself off from the world because of your anxiety. Many people mistakenly believe that accepting anxiety means limiting yourself to it, as though you've "sealed your fate." In truth, it's the opposite. Acceptance unlocks the door of anxiety's cage, freeing you to engage with the world without letting anxiety hold you back.

Acceptance is NOT inaction. On the contrary, acceptance creates space for action. By accepting anxiety, you stop fighting against it and instead start focusing on what you can do to improve your situation. This shift from resistance to action leads to "better" and "change."

Acceptance is NOT self-criticism. Acceptance fosters self-compassion. Recognizing, without judgment, that anxiety is a part of your experience helps you treat yourself with kindness and understanding. Remember, **anxiety does NOT make you "less."**

As I learned the true meaning of acceptance, I realized I was struggling with it because I was overcomplicating it! Acceptance is simple, and a concept I learned in Dialectical Behavior Therapy (DBT) captures it perfectly: **Radical Acceptance**.

Radical means "complete" or "all-encompassing." No ifs or buts, no desires or regrets, no exceptions, and no conditions. And so, to radically accept means to accept reality AS IS.

Radical Acceptance

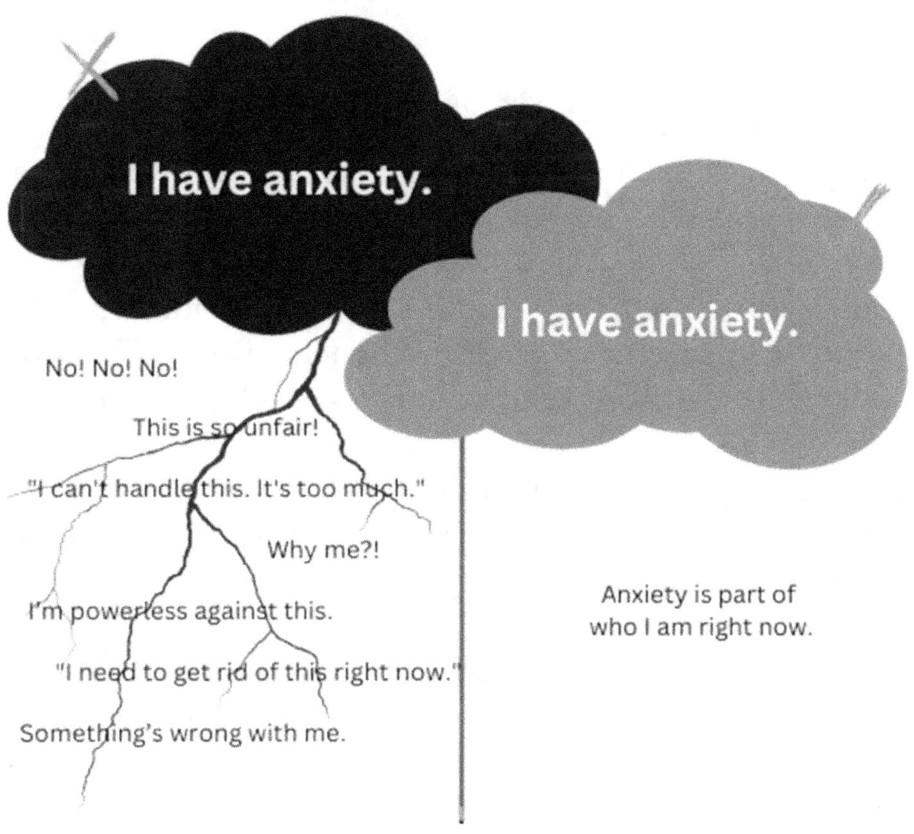

Hello dear reader,

Would you like to explore Dialectical Behavior Therapy's (DBT) Radical Acceptance? If so, I invite you to get the Amazon bestseller "The Radical Acceptance Workbook: Transform Your Life & Free Your Mind with the Healing Power of Self-Love & Compassion—Positive Lessons to Treat Anxiety, Self-Doubt, Shame & Negative Self-Judgement."

Just visit https://life-zen.com/rad-acceptance or scan this QR code.

So, what happens when you DON'T accept anxiety's presence and impact on your life? It usually means four things: you're denying, resisting, avoiding, or unaware.

- **Denying** is when you refuse to acknowledge the presence of anxiety, convincing yourself that it doesn't exist or isn't affecting you. (*Who? Me? I don't have anxiety. What are you talking about?*)

- **Avoiding** is when you try to escape or steer clear of situations that trigger anxiety, often leading to avoidance behaviors that can exacerbate the problem. (*I don't like taking elevators. Why? Oh, uh... just because.*)

- **Resisting** is when you fight against the anxiety, which can create additional stress and make the anxiety worse. (*I can push through this. I don't need help from anything or anyone.*)

- **Unaware** is when you're not giving anxiety signs and symptoms the attention they deserve. It's like ignoring the check engine light on your car. You keep driving as if everything is fine until the car breaks down unexpectedly one day.

Unfortunately, here's the problem of doing any of the above:

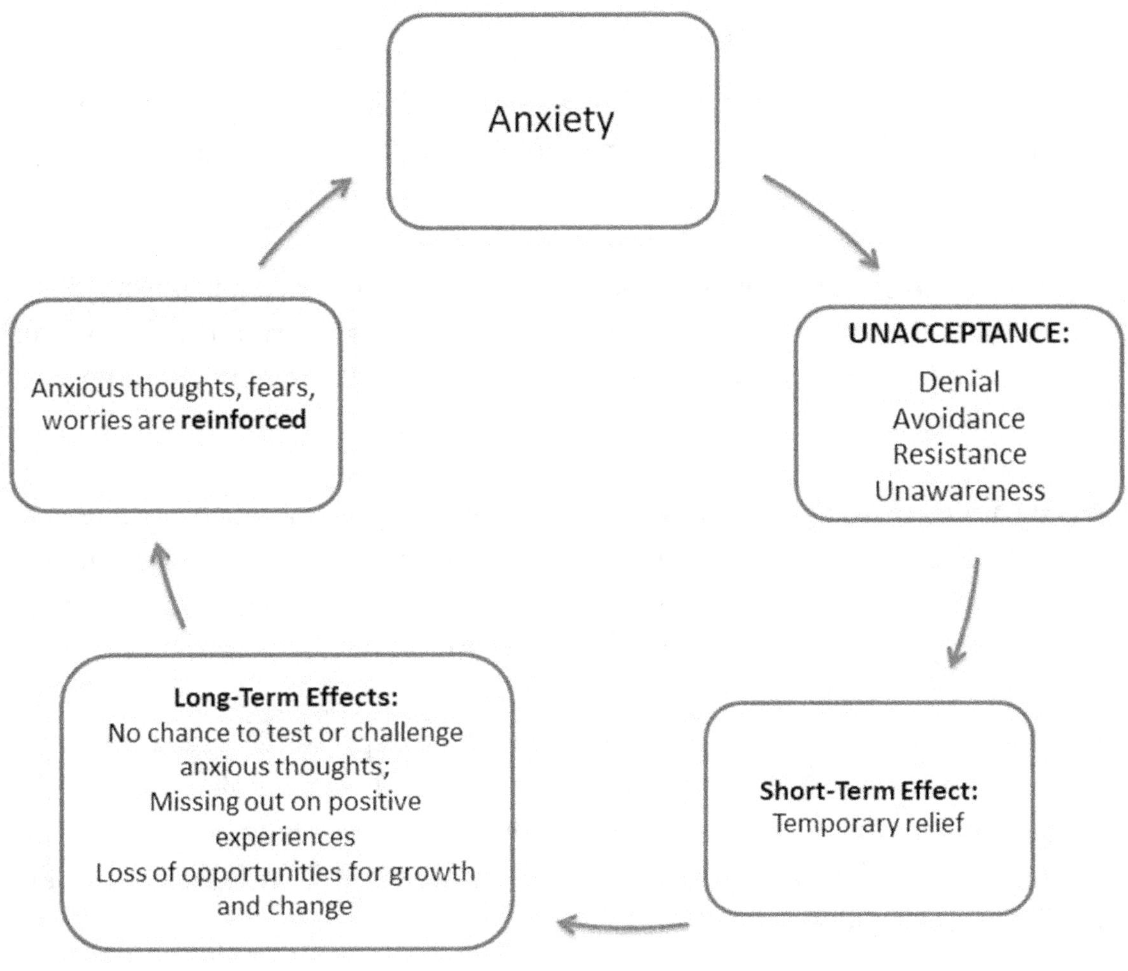

Acceptance is a very powerful and healing concept, not just for anxiety relief but for overall mental and emotional well-being. The following exercises aim to help you embrace acceptance into your life.

Worksheet 12: Acceptance Moments

If acceptance is unusual for you, this exercise will help it become more of a habit. It calls for intentionally creating moments of acceptance throughout the day.

Step 1. Morning reflection. As soon as you wake up, take a few minutes to set an intention for the day. Use acceptance statements to ground yourself. For example, "Today, I accept whatever emotions come my way and will approach them with kindness."

Step 2. Acceptance check-ins. Set reminders on your phone or calendar to pause and check in with yourself at least thrice daily (e.g., morning, midday, evening). When the reminder goes off, take a moment to pause and practice deep breathing while scanning your body for tension or discomfort.

Acknowledge any emotions or thoughts that are present. Use acceptance statements to acknowledge them without judgment. For example, "I notice I'm feeling anxious right now. It's okay to feel this way. I have a right to this emotion. But, you know what? I'm going to be okay," or "I'm feeling calm. I'm grateful for this feeling."

Step 3. Acceptance journaling. At the end of each day, take 5-10 minutes to write about your experiences. Reflect on moments when you felt anxious, angry, stressed, happy, or any other strong emotion. Here are a few journal prompts:

- *What emotions did I experience today?*
- *How did I respond to these emotions?*
- *What can I accept about my experience today?*

Example journal entry: Today, I felt really anxious before my meeting. I accept that this anxiety is part of my experience. I handled it by taking deep breaths, washing my face with cold water, and reminding myself it's okay to feel this way.

Step 4. Acceptance in action. Throughout the day, practice acceptance during various activities (e.g., during a commute, while eating, or during a break). Practice mindfulness by deliberately pausing, observing, and noting your thoughts and emotions. And whatever arises, accept them without judgment.

For example, while drinking your morning coffee, take a moment to notice its warmth, scent, and taste. Acknowledge any thoughts about the day ahead and remind yourself, "Whatever comes up, I'll be okay."

Step 5. Evening wind-down. Before bed, take a few minutes to "reflect and release" your day. **Important**: Try not to overthink or ruminate. Just go over the day and quickly acknowledge any unresolved emotions or thoughts. If it helps, use a mantra to help release any lingering stress.

Example: I did my best today. I accept what I accomplished and what I didn't. It's okay to let go and rest now.

Worksheet 13: Anxiety Acceptance Affirmations

This exercise involves creating and repeating statements that foster an attitude of acceptance toward your anxiety.

Step 1. Write down a few acceptance statements. Here are a few ideas:

[ ] I accept myself, including my anxious thoughts and feelings.

[ ] I accept that I am feeling anxious right now.

[ ] It's okay to feel this way at this moment.

[ ] I'm struggling. I accept that this is due to my anxiety.

[ ] I accept that my anxiety is part of my current experience, and that's okay.

[ ] My anxiety doesn't define me; it's just a part of what I'm experiencing right now.

[ ] It's okay to be anxious and uncertain and to not have all the answers right now.

Step 2. Repeat your acceptance statements to yourself daily, especially during anxious moments.

Step 3. Use soothing gestures like placing your hand on your heart or giving yourself a one-armed hug (i.e., place one hand over the opposite shoulder) while repeating your acceptance statements to reinforce the message.

Step 4. Practice this exercise for a few minutes daily and during heightened anxiety.

Worksheet 14: Using Acceptance to Handle Difficult Situations

This exercise aims to help you develop and practice acceptance in handling difficult situations, which can reduce their impact and help you respond more effectively.

Step 1. Identify a difficult situation. Think of a recent situation that caused you distress or discomfort, and write down a brief description.

Example: I never felt comfortable with my brother-in-law. I just feel he's always judging me. He lives overseas but was on vacation here, so my husband invited him for dinner. As soon as I found out, I couldn't sleep properly. I went into "hyper mode," obsessively planning and changing the food menu, thinking of how to rearrange the furniture, and worrying about making a fool of myself. My mind kept racing with anxious thoughts, and I felt a constant knot in my stomach. I was overwhelmed with the need to make everything perfect, fearing his judgment every step of the way.

Step 2. Observe your thoughts and feelings. Sit comfortably in a quiet place and close your eyes. Take a few deep breaths to center yourself. Recall the difficult situation you described above, and notice any changes in your body and the thoughts and feelings that arise NOW. Write them down AS IS. Don't censor yourself or analyze anything.

Example: I feel my heart racing and my palms sweating as I think about the event. I notice I'm slightly clenching my jaw. I'm getting anxious again.

Step 3. Acknowledge and accept your reactions without trying to change or judge them.

Examples:
- I accept that thinking about the situation is making me anxious right now.
- I think that whatever I did was still not enough. I accept this thought.
- I'm noticing that I'm afraid of being judged. I accept this fear as part of my current experience.

Step 4. Use mindfulness to <u>stay present</u>. Practice a short mindfulness meditation to stay present. Focus on your breath or use a guided mindfulness app (e.g., Headspace, Calm, etc.). When your mind wanders to a difficult situation, gently bring it back to the present moment. Do this for 5-10 minutes.

Step 5. After the mindfulness exercise, **take a few minutes to reflect** on the experience. Write down any insights or changes in perspective you noticed.

Example: After the mindfulness exercise, I felt calmer and more detached from the situation and my anxious thoughts. I accept that the situation is in the PAST and that I have no control over it anymore; I cannot change it, so I'll let it go with each deep exhale.

Step 6. Create an action plan. If this reflective exercise helped you identify a trigger, think of practical steps you can take the next time you face a similar difficult situation. Write down these steps and how you will use acceptance to handle the situation. (If you didn't identify any trigger, that's okay too.)

Example: I think I've always known deep inside that my brother-in-law is one of my anxiety triggers. I accept this fully now. I don't have an "action plan" for this yet, but my first step is to talk to my husband. I'll communicate that I prefer to limit contact with my brother-in-law as I go through my anxiety relief journey. I want to be better at managing my anxiety in general before addressing my brother-in-law.

Step 7. Celebrate yourself for facing and accepting your difficult emotions with simple, positive gestures. For example, engage in a favorite activity, treat yourself to a favorite snack or beverage, etc.

Chapter 6: Cognitive Defusion

"You don't have to control your thoughts. You just have to stop letting them control you." – Dan Millman

Do you remember the <u>What Causes Anxiety</u> table on page 19? Although there is no exact data available, it's widely believed that *psychological factors* such as cognitive distortions (e.g., negative thinking patterns, mind traps, etc.) contribute significantly to many of today's mental health issues, including anxiety. (Correcting or modifying cognitive distortions is the main focus of CBT).

I don't know about you, but I don't recall a single positive thought whenever I experience anxiety. Most anxious thoughts are negative or, at the very least, unhelpful. They often involve worrying about potential dangers, failures, or negative outcomes, which leads to predominantly negative thinking patterns.

Here are just some of the most common beliefs or thinking patterns that people with anxiety disorders have:

Generalized Anxiety Disorder (GAD)	Specific Phobias (e.g., fear of heights, animals, flying, etc.)
I'm not good enough. *I'm unlovable.* *I'm always going to fail.* *I'm a burden to others.* *I'm weak.* *I'm not deserving of happiness.* *I'm a disappointment.* *I'm going to embarrass myself.*	*If I encounter [the phobic object or situation], something terrible will happen.* *I won't be able to handle it if I face [the phobic object or situation].* *I need to avoid [phobic object or situation] because it's extremely dangerous, and I will get hurt or even die.*

I'm going to mess everything up. I'm broken.	I will LOSE IT if I'm near [the phobic object or situation]. No one understands how frightening [the phobic object or situation] is to me.
Social Anxiety Disorder (SAD, or Social Phobia)	**Panic Disorder**
Everyone is judging me. I will embarrass myself. People will think I'm weird or awkward. I will say something stupid. I cannot handle social situations at all.	I'm losing control. I'm going crazy. I'm going to die during a panic attack. I can't breathe. I'm having a heart attack.
Agoraphobia	**Separation Anxiety Disorder**
I won't be able to escape if something goes wrong. Help won't be available if I need it. I'll lose control in public. No place is safe. Crowded places are dangerous.	Something bad will happen if I'm not with my loved one. I can't handle being alone. I'm going to be alone because I deserve it. I'll never see them again if they leave. They're going to leave me. They're going to leave me. They're going to leave me. They won't come back.
Selective Mutism	**Health Anxiety** (Hypochondriasis)
People will judge me if I speak. I never find the right words. It's safer to stay quiet.	I'm going to die from this. Doctors are missing something. Every symptom means something is

I will embarrass myself if I speak up.	*wrong.*
No one in this world wants to hear what I have to say.	*I need constant reassurance about my health.*
	I have a serious illness.
Substance/Medication-Induced Anxiety Disorder	**Anxiety Disorder Due to Another Medical Condition** (e.g., heart disease, chronic pain, etc.)
This substance is making me anxious. *Withdrawal symptoms will never go away.* *I can't control my anxiety without medication.* *My anxiety will get worse if I stop using.* *I'm not normal without my meds.*	*I'm terrified I won't be able to work anymore because of my illness.* *What if I never get better?* *I'm in pain. I'll always be in pain.* *I can't manage.* *I'm scared. Always scared. What if there's no cure? What if I use up all my savings? What if I end up alone with no one to care for me?*

Our thoughts are very powerful. Science proves that how we think and feel colors our entire experience of physical reality.[36,37,38]

In CBT, the relationship between our thoughts, our emotions, and our behaviors is emphasized. This concept is called the *cognitive triangle*. More specifically, it aims to explain how our thoughts influence how we feel, which subsequently influences how we act, which then influences (or rather reinforces) our thoughts. On and on it goes...

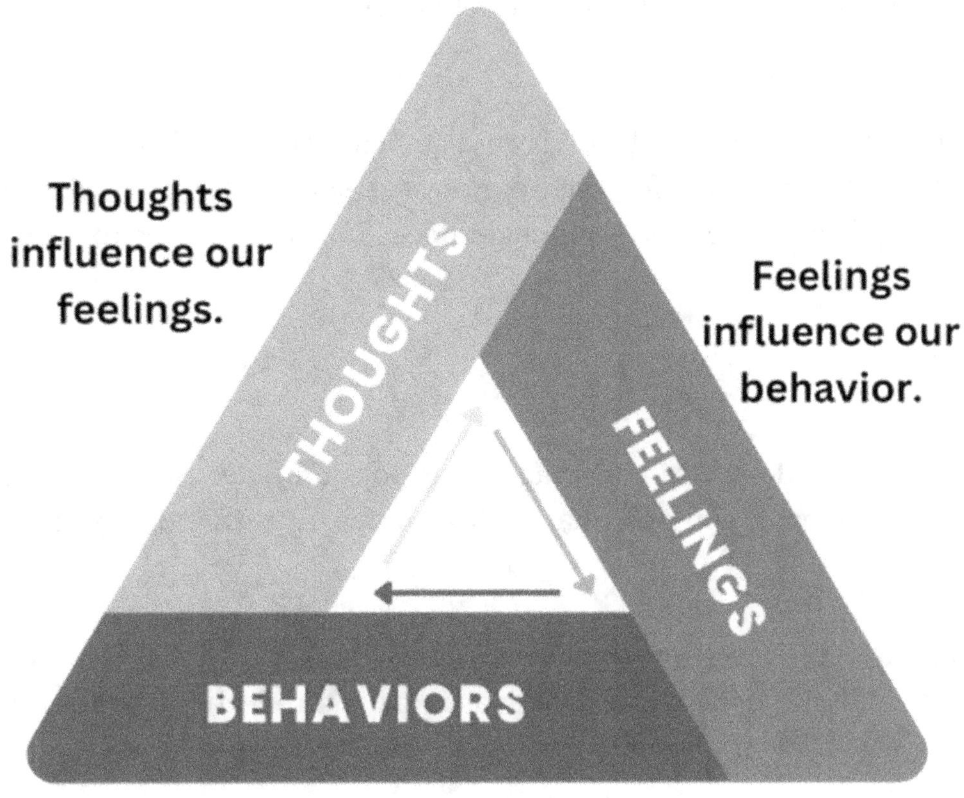

As you can see in the above image, anxiety is like a self-fulfilling prophesy. That's why, **when it comes to anxiety**, it's important to remember this: **don't believe your thoughts**. Why not? Because anxiety is generally considered to be an emotional response, not a logical one.

Now, as I always say, your emotions are valid. Nothing and no one should discredit your feelings. But... what if your *thoughts* are invalid? What if they're somehow distorted or misaligned from reality? THIS is the point of Cognitive Defusion.

Cognitive Defusion encourages you to detach, unglue, or unhook yourself from negative, unhelpful, unproductive, and unverified thoughts. By doing this, you break the cycle of the *cognitive triangle*, opening the door to new or alternative emotions and subsequent behaviors, ultimately leading to anxiety relief.

Further, cognitive defusion focuses on distancing yourself from your anxious thoughts and seeing them for what they are—JUST THOUGHTS (not reality). Besides, just because you have a thought doesn't mean you need to think about it.

Thoughts vs. Thinking

Thoughts are random ideas or images that pop into your mind (i.e., internal mental distractions). You don't have much control over them; they appear and disappear.

Thinking is a *process* of consciously engaging with your thoughts. It's deliberate and purposeful, involving reasoning and reflection. And because it's deliberate, you have more control over thinking because it involves active effort and focus.

So, bottom-line, thoughts are like clouds that drift into your mind without you doing anything. Thinking is deciding to shape those clouds into something meaningful.

When it comes to anxiety relief, it's important to understand this difference because now you know that not every anxiety-driven thought needs to be acted upon.

It takes practice to see your thoughts as just thoughts or uninvited mental events. The following exercises are designed to help you with this.

Worksheet 15: Cognitive Defusion Gameboard

Create psychological distance between your thoughts and yourself using the Cognitive Defusion Gameboard below. By using an interactive exercise, you can make the practice of *defusion* more engaging and enjoyable. Now, keep an open mind, okay? Some activities may come across as "quirky," but just try them. As I often say, you'll never know what works until you try one that might.

Step 1. Gameboard. Print the gameboard image below or draw a similar one on a piece of paper or digital drawing tool.

Step 2. Game pieces. Get a small token to move around the board (a coin, a button, a chess piece, or any small object). You will also need a die to decide which technique to do and how many spaces to move.

Step 3. Instructions.
- Place your token on the starting point of the gameboard.
- Roll the die to determine how many spaces to move your token. Move the token accordingly.
- Based on the space you land on, practice the cognitive defusion technique mentioned on it.
- After practicing the defusion technique, take a moment to reflect on how you feel. Notice any changes in your anxiety levels or your perspective on the thought.
- IF you're still anxious, roll the die again and move your token to the next technique. Repeat the process of practicing the technique and reflecting on your experience until you feel relief.

START 1	2 Labeling Thoughts	3 Metaphors	4 Silly Voices	5 Thank Your Mind
10 Repetition	9 Thoughts ON Objects	8 Breathing with Thoughts	7 Objectify the Thought I	6 Writing & Observing
11 Objectify the Thought II	12 Musical Thoughts	CHOOSE! 13 Do whatever technique you want today.	14 Mindful Acknowledgment	15 Storytelling
20 Labeling Thoughts	19 Metaphors	18 Silly Voices	17 Thank Your Mind	16 Repetition
21 Thoughts ON Objects	22 Breathing with Thoughts	23 Objectify the Thought I	24 Writing & Observing	25 Objectify the Thought II
26 Musical Thoughts	27 Mindful Acknowledgment	28 Storytelling	FINISH Go and celebrate. You deserve it!	

> **Labeling Thoughts.** When a negative thought arises, label it as a thought rather than a fact. For example, instead of "I'm going to die," say, "I'm having the THOUGHT that I'm going to die."

> **Metaphors.** Visualize your thoughts in a way that helps you see them as separate from yourself. For example, imagine your thoughts as leaves floating down a stream or clouds passing by in the sky.

- ➤ **Silly Voices.** Say your negative thoughts out loud in a silly or exaggerated voice. For example, repeat "I'm a failure" in the voice of a cartoon character. This can make the thought seem less serious and impactful. (*Just sharing: I like doing this using a Minion-type voice.*)

- ➤ **Thank Your Mind.** Acknowledge your thoughts without letting them control you. For example, when a negative thought arises, say, "Thanks, mind. That's an interesting thought."

- ➤ **Repetition.** Repeat the thought out loud or in your head until it loses meaning and becomes just a series of sounds. For example, repeat "I'm going to get trapped in an elevator" repeatedly until it feels like a nonsensical string of words.

- ➤ **Thoughts ON Objects.** Imagine placing your thoughts on various objects and watching them move away. For example, picture an anxious thought as a balloon drifting into the sky, a car driving away, or your pet cat running away from you.

- ➤ **Writing and Observing.** Write down your thoughts and observe them as if you were an outsider. For example, write "Everyone is looking at me and judging me" on a piece of paper. Look at the paper and remind yourself that it's just a thought, not a fact. Next, crumple the paper and throw it in the trash can.

- ➤ **Breathing with Thoughts.** Use your breath to help create distance from your thoughts. For example, practice <u>Mindful Breathing</u> on page 55.

- ➤ **Objectify the Thought I.** Turn the thought into an object. Visualize your thought as a physical object, like a rock or a pen. Name it (or not), see it as separate from yourself, and then move on.

Just sharing: Peanut butter. I swear I don't know where it came from. I was having anxious thoughts, and the words "peanut butter" popped into my head. I didn't question or analyze it; I just went with it. So, whenever anxiety would start, I'd say something like, "Well, "peanut butter" entered my mind again" or "Hmmm, peanut butter" or "Hi peanut butter". I wouldn't voice out or explain the thought; I just called it peanut butter. And for some weird reason, the grip of my anxious thought would loosen.

➤ **Objectify the Thought II.** Turn the thought into an object. Visualize your thoughts as a physical object, like a rock or a coffee mug. Look at it, examine it, and see it as separate from yourself.

Maxene[1], a close friend of mine whose anxiety went from bad to worse after going through divorce trauma, has this to share.

"I was blindsided by my divorce. On my side, I thought we were A-Okay. And then, one day, he just sat me down and... left. I already had GAD, but it was manageable. After the divorce, I spiraled. That was three years, countless therapy and counseling sessions, and a round of anti-anxiety meds that gave me severe withdrawal symptoms ago.

Anyway... when I learned about objectifying thoughts, I bought a goldfish for this very purpose. Whenever I sensed anxiety looming, I would look at that goldfish and imagine it as my anxiety. (I didn't name it, so it remained detached from me.)

I don't know why, but it worked. Physically seeing the goldfish helped me objectify my anxious thoughts, making them seem external and manageable rather than an internal and overwhelming part of myself."

➤ **Musical Thoughts.** Sing your negative thoughts to the tune of a familiar song. For example, sing "I can't do this. I'm going to fail" to the tune of "Twinkle, Twinkle Little Star."

➤ **Mindful Acknowledgment.** Recognize the thought without trying to change or judge it. For example, when you think a negative thought such as "Everyone is belittling me," say to yourself, "I notice I'm having the thought that..."

> **Storytelling.** Turn your negative thoughts into a story with a beginning, middle, and end. This will help you see your negative thoughts as just ONE possible interpretation. (Note: This technique might take some time, but you don't have to finish your story in one go. It can be a work in progress as long as doing so provides relief.)

Here's a sample short story based on the anxious thought, "I don't feel safe in this world."

--- *The Beginning* ---

Emily had always felt a creeping sense of danger lurking around every corner. Every news story about a crime or disaster seemed to confirm her fears: the world is a dangerous place. This anxiety kept her indoors, far away from the unknown variables of the outside world.

--- *The Middle* ---

One day, a power outage struck her neighborhood. Emily was struck with anxiety, but she didn't go out. After all, she ensured she had enough supplies for at least a week. However, the lack of power meant Emily couldn't get online by Day 3 (she had already exhausted all her devices' power). By the end of the week, Emily was starting to feel loneliness like she never felt before.

By the end of the following week, Emily forced herself out of her apartment in search of light, warmth, water, and any contact. She ventured to a nearby community center where neighbors gathered with candles and flashlights. There, Emily met Alex, a volunteer who noticed her discomfort and started a gentle conversation. Alex shared stories about his travels around the world, describing not just the challenges but the incredible kindness of strangers he'd encountered.

As Alex talked about his tales, Emily began to think, "How can this man be so OUT there and feel so safe and happy? He doesn't look fearful in the least of the unknown." Emily questioned whether the world might hold more safety than she had realized.

--- *The End* ---

Over time, Emily decided to challenge her fears. She started small, visiting the library and nearby local parks because they were quiet and peaceful.

She then visited a small coffee shop about a block from where she lived, where Emily discovered peaceful moments, a few friendly faces, and the most amazing croissant sandwich she had ever eaten! (Part of her was thinking, "I've been missing this?!")

Each positive experience built her confidence, slowly reshaping her belief about the world's dangers. Emily and Alex kept in touch, and two years later, she joined him on a volunteer trip abroad, finding a sense of safety not in isolation but in the shared humanity and kindness of the people she met. Emily also realized that the world hadn't changed, but her interpretation of it had transformed.

Worksheet 16: Deal with Real

Did you know our brains can't distinguish between what's real and what's not? Studies show that our brains often respond to real and imagined scenarios with the same intensity.[39,40,41] This is why, even when we logically understand that our fears or worries might not happen, we still tend to react to them (in both emotion and behavior) as if they're real.

Does this mean we're all just walking around, incapable of knowing what's real and what's not? No. Humans have a sort of built-in "reality threshold." If a signal or stimulus crosses this threshold, the brain logs it as "real;" if it doesn't, it files it under "imagined."[42]

The "reality threshold" usually works because most imagined signals are faint. Unfortunately, this is not the case for those who suffer from anxiety. Our imagined signals are so intense they *cross* the reality threshold, making us mistake them for reality.

This following exercise aims to help you successfully detach or defuse from anxious thoughts and get you to focus on facts or what's real.

Step 1. Identify your anxious thoughts. Sit in a quiet place with a pen and notebook. Close your eyes and take a few deep breaths to calm yourself. Next, write down the thoughts that are causing your anxiety. Be as specific as you can.

Example: I'm consumed with financial worries. I'm afraid I'm going to go bankrupt and end up homeless.

Step 2. Emotion check-in. On a scale of 1 to 10 (1 being the lowest and 10 being the highest), how intense is your anxiety right now? Encircle your answer.

1	2	3	4	5	6	7	8	9	10

Step 3. Label your anxious thoughts. Read the thoughts you wrote down, and then say any of the following to yourself:

[ ] This is a thought, not a fact.
[ ] This is a passing thought. It doesn't need mental energy or intention.
[ ] I'm having a THOUGHT. I don't need to think about it.
[ ] This is just a thought I'm having. It doesn't define me.
[ ] This is a thought, a mental event. It's not my current reality.
[ ] This is an uninvited thought. I don't need to have a conversation with it.

Step 4. Visualize the thought as an object. Choose an object representing your thought (e.g., rock, leaf, cup, etc.). Imagine holding the object in your hand, examining it from all angles. This step helps you look at the thought with detached curiosity.

Step 5. Examine the evidence. Next, you will differentiate between thoughts and facts by examining the evidence. Write down as much evidence as possible *for* and *against* each thought.

Anxious Thoughts	What evidence *supports* this thought?	What evidence *contradicts* this thought?
Example: I'm going to go bankrupt.	*Example: I don't have any savings.*	*Example:* *- I have a stable job with a regular income.* *- I have a friend good with finances and can*

Anxious Thoughts	What evidence *supports* this thought?	What evidence *contradicts* this thought?
		help give me budgeting tips.

Step 6. Emotion check-in. Do your emotions match the *facts* of the situation, or do they match your *assumptions* of the situation? Encircle your answer.

FACTS	ASSUMPTIONS

On a scale of 1 to 10 (1 being the lowest and 10 being the highest), how intense is your anxiety right now? Encircle your answer.

1	2	3	4	5	6	7	8	9	10

Hopefully, you can feel less intense emotions by taking a step back and writing down evidence for and against your anxious thoughts. If not, that's okay too. Remember, your emotions are always valid.

Step 7. Reframe. Replace each negative and unhelpful thought with a more balanced, fact-based perspective.

Anxious Thought	Is this thought helpful? Why or why not?	What's a more realistic, fact-based way to look at this situation?
Example: I'm going to go bankrupt.	*Example: NO. I just get more anxious when I think about this.*	*Example: I may not have any savings now, but having a stable job means I can tighten my belt and put away a little something starting my next paycheck.*

Anxious Thought	Is this thought helpful? Why or why not?	What's a more realistic, fact-based way to look at this situation?

Step 8. Take a little break to focus on the present moment. Practice mindfulness by focusing on your current surroundings. Use your senses to notice:

- FIVE things you can see,
- FOUR things you can hear,
- THREE things you can touch or feel,
- TWO things you can smell and
- ONE thing you can taste.

Step 9. Create an action plan. When we're anxious, we get stuck in a place of worry. Shifting your mind from "worry" to "solution" helps break the anxiety cycle and empowers you to take control of the situation. So, identify specific steps you can take to address the issue or mitigate its impact. This proactive approach reduces anxiety and fosters a sense of accomplishment and confidence!

Anxious Thought	What can I do right now?	What can I do in the near future?
Example: I'm going to go bankrupt.	*Example:* *- Sit down and create a budget.*	*Example:* *- Look for additional sources of income.*

Anxious Thought	What can I do right now?	What can I do in the near future?
	- *Go through my stuff and identify at least three things I can sell online or to family and friends.*	- *Consult a financial advisor.*

Important: If you can't fill this table out just yet, that's okay. You might find that the best thing you can do right now is to simply process steps 1-6 above or talk to someone for help or advice. The important thing is to start training your mind to focus on present facts and reality.

Chapter 7: Self as Context

"It is the mark of an educated mind to be able to entertain a thought without accepting it." – Aristotle

Self as Context is a skill that helps you see yourself separate from your thoughts, feelings, and experiences. It's about understanding that **you're MORE than the anxious contents of your mind**.

Cognitive Defusion vs. Self as Context

Many are confused by these two core skills in ACT, so let me quickly differentiate them here.

Cognitive defusion involves distancing yourself from your thoughts to see them as just thoughts, not truths. Self as context refers to the perspective of viewing yourself as the observer of your experiences rather than being defined by them.

Cognitive Defusion

Consumed by anxiety.

Hmmm, I'm noticing that I'm having anxious thoughts.

Self as Context

"Being" anxiety.

Observing anxiety.

Separating one's self from one's own thoughts isn't easy, all the more so for people with anxiety. For one, anxious thoughts can feel like warnings of danger, making it hard to ignore or detach from them. They also often come with a high "emotional charge," which makes the thought feel more intense and thus harder to let go. Lastly, anxiety is not a one-time event. We often experience the same thought patterns over and over, creating a cycle that's hard to break.

But as you know by now, beliefs and thoughts rooted in anxiety can be damaging in the long run. Remember, you're NOT your thoughts, but think of them long enough, and they can be.

For instance, if you think you are unlovable, you might start to view yourself as terrible or disgusting. Similarly, if your thoughts constantly revolve around "getting sick," you might begin to see yourself as an "ill person" and even start to exhibit symptoms of the illness you fear. (This is similar to the *nocebo effect*, where negative expectations can lead to negative health outcomes, much like the opposite of the placebo effect.)

So, it's not just important to unglue yourself from your anxious thoughts and feelings (*cognitive defusion*) but to clearly see them as something completely separate from your person.

> **You have thoughts. You are NOT your thoughts.**
> **You experience emotions. You are NOT your emotions.**

If you're NOT your thoughts and emotions, who are you then? You're an **observer** of them. It's the "you" that's noticing what's going through your mind.

Now, your thoughts and feelings change frequently. However, "you," the observer (Observer Self) remains consistent. It's the stable part of you that experiences all your mental and emotional states.

It's important to identify as the "Observer Self" so that you realize that your anxious thoughts and feelings are separate from who you are as a person. So, instead of saying or thinking, "I'm invisible," you can say or think, "I notice that I'm feeling invisible." This shift helps you see anxiety as something that you're experiencing, not something that defines you.

Also, something amazing happens when you identify as the "Observer Self." You start to see anxiety as something you can manage better because it's "separate" from you. And because they're separate, they become less overwhelming. You might even become curious about it! For example, suppose you're overwhelmed and start thinking, "I cannot handle this!"

Without Self as Context, you might feel completely engulfed by this thought, believing it fully and thus exacerbating your anxiety.

With Self as Context, you go, "Hmmm, I'm having the thought I can't handle this." This acknowledgment helps you see the thought as a temporary experience. You realize that while the thought is present, it doesn't define your capability or who you are. Observer Self remains calm and detached, enabling you to consider ways to manage anxiety without being overwhelmed by it.

The following exercises are all designed to help you see yourself as the Observer Self whenever you experience anxiety.

Worksheet 17: The Movie in My Mind

Step 1. Find a comfortable place to sit where you won't be disturbed. Take a few deep, calming breaths to center yourself.

Step 2. Close your eyes and **notice your thoughts** as they come and go.

Step 3. Shift to the Observer Self by imagining sitting in a movie theater, watching your thoughts play out on the screen. You are the observer, <u>not</u> the actor.

Step 4. After a few minutes, open your eyes and **reflect** on the experience. Notice how you could observe your thoughts without being caught up in them.

Step 5. Journal (optional). Write down your thoughts during the exercise and describe how observing it from a distance felt.

Example: I thought about how alone I feel since the divorce. I always think of the phrase, "I don't see a future anymore." However, observing my thoughts like a movie made me realize that while my feelings of loneliness and despair are real, it doesn't define my entire existence. In my "movie," I saw my 11-year-old daughter and remembered that I still have meaningful connections. This helped me feel less overwhelmed and more hopeful about building a new chapter in my life.

Worksheet 18: The Lighthouse

Imagine that you're a lighthouse standing tall and firm on the shore. It remains steady and strong despite the changing weather and turbulent waves around it. Your thoughts and feelings are like the weather and waves—they come and go, but you, as the lighthouse, remain constant.

Step 1. Find a quiet place where you can sit comfortably without distractions. Take a few deep breaths to center yourself and prepare for the visualization.

Step 2. Create a vivid mental image of the lighthouse. Close your eyes and picture a lighthouse standing tall on the shore. Visualize its strong foundation, tall structure, and the bright light it emits to guide ships safely through the storm. Imagine the waves crashing against the lighthouse and the weather changing, but the lighthouse stands firm and unaffected.

Step 3. Identify and accept your anxious thoughts and feelings. Think about your current anxieties and worries. What thoughts and feelings are causing you distress? Write them down or mentally note them.

Example: I am worried about my job security.

Step 4. Connect your thoughts and feelings to the weather and waves. Imagine each of your anxious thoughts and feelings as different weather conditions or waves crashing against the lighthouse. For example, your worries could be represented by a stormy sky. Acknowledge these thoughts and feelings without judgment, just as the lighthouse acknowledges the weather and waves without being affected by them.

Step 5. Internalize the perspective of being the lighthouse. Remind yourself that you are the lighthouse—steady, strong, and constant. Your anxious thoughts and feelings are temporary and external, like the weather and waves. Say to yourself, "I am the lighthouse. My thoughts and feelings are like the weather and waves—they come and go, but I remain steady and strong."

Step 6. When you're ready, open your eyes and take a few moments to reflect on how the visualization made you feel. Write down any insights or feelings of calmness and strength that you experienced.

Example: I felt less overwhelmed by my worries. The lighthouse visualization helped me see my thoughts and feelings as temporary and external.

Whenever you feel overwhelmed by anxiety, take a moment to visualize the lighthouse. Remember that you are the lighthouse; your thoughts and feelings are like the weather and waves—*they will pass.*

Worksheet 19: The Chessboard

Imagine your mind as a chessboard; chess pieces are your thoughts and feelings. The pieces can be black or white, representing negative and positive thoughts and feelings. Just like playing chess in real life, remember that the chessboard holds all these pieces but is not affected by the game itself. It simply provides the space for the game to unfold.

Step 1. Find a quiet place where you can sit comfortably without distractions. Take a few deep breaths to center yourself and prepare for the visualization.

Step 2. Recognize and categorize your thoughts and feelings as chess pieces. Think about any recent (or current) anxious thoughts and feelings. Write them down. Label each thought or feeling as either a black piece (negative) or a white piece (positive). (This step alone helps with anxiety because it makes you realize that negative AND positive thoughts and emotions exist.)

Example:
I'm scared of failing (black piece).
I felt proud of my work yesterday (white piece).

Step 3. Visualize your thoughts and feelings as pieces on a chessboard. On a piece of paper, draw a simple chessboard or imagine one in your mind. Place each thought or feeling on the chessboard. See them as separate pieces on the board. Visualize the black and white pieces moving around, sometimes in conflict, sometimes in harmony.

Here's an example:

The Chessboard

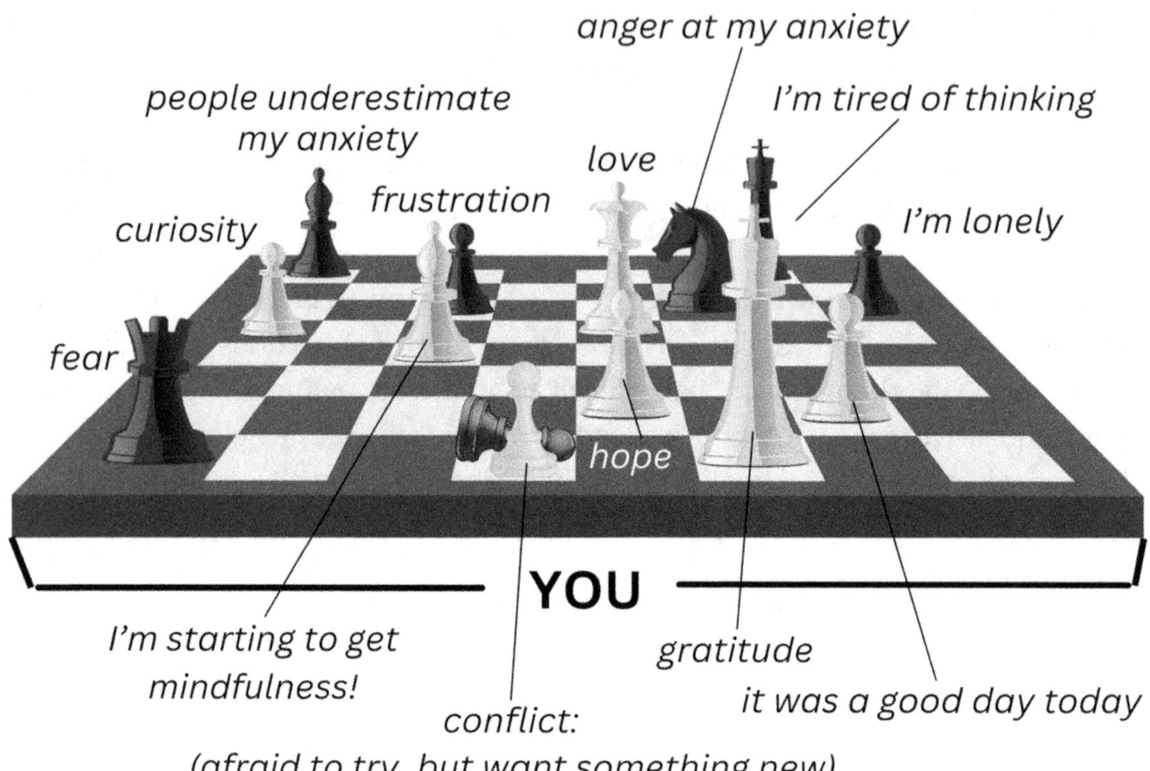

Step 4. Recognize that the chessboard is you (your mind). Realize that you, as the observer of your thoughts and feelings, are like the chessboard. You hold all these thoughts and feelings (chess pieces), but they DO NOT define you. Say to yourself, "I am the chessboard. I can hold all my thoughts and feelings without being controlled by them."

Step 5. Observe without judging. Whenever an anxious thought or feeling arises, just place it on the chessboard in your mind. Watch it without judgment. Remember, the pieces may move, be added, or disappear... but the chessboard remains steady and unaffected.

Worksheet 20: Self as Context Journal

Step 1. Create a dedicated space for your Self as Context journal. You can use a notebook, journal, digital document, etc. Divide each page into two columns: "Observed Thoughts and Feelings" and "Observing Self."

Step 2. Set aside 10-15 minutes to reflect at the end of each day. In the "Observed Thoughts and Feelings" column, write down any anxious thoughts or feelings you experienced during the day. In the "Observing Self" column, write about your experience of having these thoughts and feelings.

Observed Thoughts and Feelings	Observing Self
Example: *I felt a panic attack come on as my partner was leaving this morning.*	*Example:* *I noticed that I had a lot of worries about them cheating or being abandoned as they were leaving. I observed this worry and felt it in my chest. I also felt my jaw clenching. I then took a deep breath and told myself, "I am not my worry; I am the one noticing it. I am having an uninvited mental event. This is not my reality."*

Observed Thoughts and Feelings	Observing Self

Step 3. Observe without judging. As you write in your journal, practice observing your thoughts and feelings without judging them as good or bad. Simply note their presence and your experience of observing them.

Step 4. Reflect on any patterns and insights. At the end of each week, review your journal entries. Look for patterns in your anxious thoughts and feelings and how your Observing Self responded to them. Write a summary of any insights or patterns you noticed.

Example: This week, I observed that my anxiety often spikes in the morning. It begins when my partner gets ready for work and intensifies when they leave. I realized that maybe it's because I'm the one literally being left behind that triggers my anxiety. Now that I'm noticing this pattern, I think maybe I should shift to going to the gym most mornings. Maybe "getting ready" and "leaving" at the same time helps.

Step 5. Continue and express gratitude. Review your journal and reflect on your progress at the end of each month. Write a note of appreciation to yourself for the effort you've put into managing your anxiety.

Example: I'm proud of consistently journaling and observing my thoughts and feelings. I can see how this practice is helping me feel more in control and less defined by my anxiety.

Worksheet 21: Me, Them, and The Observer

This exercise will help you get anxiety relief by encouraging a sense of detachment through examining your anxious thoughts and sensations from multiple perspectives or viewpoints. The goal is to realize that your thoughts or what you fear are not the only possible outcomes in real life.

Step 1. Create a dedicated space for your Perspective-Taking exercise. You can use a notebook, journal, digital document, etc. Divide each page into three columns: "Me," "Them," and "Observer."

Step 2. Recall a recent event that caused anxiety, and then describe this event from the following points of view:

- **Me**: Describe the situation from your own perspective.
- **Them**: Describe the same situation from the perspective of someone else involved. This could be a friend, family member, or even a stranger present during the event. Write down what you imagine their thoughts, feelings, and reactions might have been.
- **Observer**: Describe the same situation from the perspective of an impartial observer, someone outside looking in and watching the event unfold. This observer has no emotional attachment to the situation. Write down what this person might see and think.

Event/Situation: *Team building weekend with colleagues.*		
Me	**Them**	**Observer**
Example: I woke up really anxious that Saturday. I just felt that something really bad was going to happen.	*Example: When I arrived at work, my colleague Ben joined me in the elevator.*	*Example: The Observer saw two people walk into an elevator...*
But I went anyway. Otherwise, thoughts of losing my job would	*He seemed calm and talked about how good this weekend would be for the team, that we all deserved to have fun, etc.*	*One was quiet. The other was talking animatedly about a team-building activity. The Observer thought, "That might be*

consume me over the weekend. *At work, I took the elevator to the 17th floor, but in my head, I was thinking…* *I'd probably say something wrong and embarrass myself in front of everyone. What if I can't participate in the activities? I'll be humiliated, and no one will take me seriously at work!*	*He didn't seem to notice my anxiety at all.*	*fun."*

Event/Situation:

Me	Them	Observer

Step 3. Reflect on the different perspectives. Read through each section of your writing. Reflect on how each perspective provides a different view of the same event. Next, consider how anxiety might influence your perspective while the other perspectives provide a more balanced view.

Example: Reading through the "Them" and "Observer" sections, I realize that my intense fear was not shared by my colleague or noticed by the observer.

Whenever you feel anxious about a situation, pause and try to view it from the perspectives of "Me," "Them," and "Observer." This practice will help you detach from your immediate anxious reaction and see the situation more clearly.

Chapter 8: Values Clarification

"When your values are clear to you, making decisions becomes easier." - Roy E. Disney

Values clarification is identifying and understanding what is most important to you. Your values guide your actions, reflect what you stand for, and give your life meaning and purpose.

I've come to realize that time really does pass quickly. When I experienced my burnout and breakdown, I was a 30-something someone. The weird part was recognizing that I wasn't *deliberate* about who I became. It was like life "just happened," and I woke up one day as "Ava." I know I'm not alone in this.

As children, we often adopt our parents' values as our own. When we venture out into the world, we tend to live by the values imposed by society. In relationships, we frequently prioritize other people's expectations and desires above our own. And what about the values imposed on us by cultural norms, educational institutions, or workplace environments? All of these make it challenging to discern what truly matters to us as individuals.

Important: This is not about assigning blame to others or judging ourselves for being influenced by external values. Instead, it's about recognizing how these influences shape us and taking the proactive step to identify and embrace our own values. Now is the time to look *inward* and figure out what values YOU consider important at this stage in your life.

What does clarifying your values have to do with anxiety?! If you don't know what's important to you, it can cause or feed your anxiety because:

- **You lack direction and purpose.** Without clear values, you might feel aimless or directionless, unsure of what you want to achieve or where to go. This lack of direction can create a sense of uncertainty and instability, which fuels anxiety. When you don't know what you stand for or what you're working towards, every decision can feel overwhelming.

- **You often feel stressed and conflicted.** Values help guide your decisions and actions. Without them, you might find yourself in situations that conflict with your innate subconscious beliefs or desires. This internal conflict can lead to stress and anxiety as you struggle to reconcile your actions with your undefined values. For example, you might take on a job or relationship that doesn't align with your true self, leading to chronic dissatisfaction and anxiety.

- **You find it difficult to make decisions.** Clear values provide a framework for making decisions. When you don't know your values, even small decisions can become paralyzing. This constant indecision and second-guessing can increase anxiety because you might always be worried about making the wrong choice and its potential consequences.

- **You're not living authentically.** Living according to others' expectations rather than your own values can create an inauthentic life. This can lead to anxiety because you feel a disconnect or mismatch between your true self and the life you are living. Over time, this can result in feelings of emptiness and anxiety.

- **You may develop low self-esteem and self-worth.** When your actions and life path don't align with your values, it can affect how you view yourself. This misalignment can lead to feelings of inadequacy and low self-worth, which are closely linked to anxiety. You might feel like you're not living up to your potential or being true to yourself.

- **Avoidance behavior might become your norm.** Without clear values, you might avoid situations that require you to confront your true desires and beliefs. This avoidance can lead to increased anxiety over time because you're not addressing the root causes of your discomfort. Avoiding difficult decisions or conversations prevents personal growth and perpetuates a cycle of anxiety.

So, HOW do you clarify your values?

Firstly, I find that it's futile to keep looking at the past and trying to figure out where things went "wrong." It's a waste of time. Yes, reflecting on past mistakes and experiences and learning from them is beneficial. However, ruminating about the past and constantly wondering "what if" isn't helpful. (Remember, you cannot undo the past.) So, when clarifying your values, focus on who you are NOW and what you hope to achieve in the future. The exercises in this chapter are designed to help you do just that.

Important: Approach the following exercises with curiosity. Don't see them as tasks or responsibilities. View them as an exciting journey into self-discovery!

Worksheet 22: Discovering Values Using Values Cards

Step 1. Print. Print out the Values Cards table below and cut out each value. Please feel free to add more if you want to.

ACCEPTANCE	ACCOUNTABILITY	AUTHENTICITY
embracing oneself and others as they are, without judgment	taking responsibility for one's actions and decisions	being true to oneself and living in alignment with one's values, beliefs, and identity
BALANCE	**CALMNESS**	**CARING**
finding equilibrium between work, relationships, and self-care	maintaining a state of tranquility and peace of mind	showing kindness and concern for others
COMMITMENT	**COMPASSION**	**CONFIDENCE**
dedication to pursuing one's goals and values	showing empathy and understanding towards others	believing in one's abilities and self-worth
CONNECTION	**CONSISTENCY**	**CONTENTMENT**
building and maintaining meaningful relationships	acting in a reliable and predictable manner	finding satisfaction and happiness in the present moment
COURAGE	**CREATIVITY**	**DEPENDABILITY**
facing challenges and fears with bravery	using imagination and innovation to express oneself	being reliable and trustworthy

DETERMINATION persistently pursuing one's goals despite obstacles	**EMPATHY** understanding and sharing the feelings of others	**ENCOURAGEMENT** supporting and uplifting yourself and others
FAIRNESS treating others with equity and justice	**FLEXIBILITY** adapting to new circumstances and situations	**FORGIVENESS** letting go of resentment and freeing yourself from negative thoughts and emotions
GRATITUDE recognizing and appreciating the positives in life	**GROWTH** striving for personal development and self-improvement	**HARMONY** creating a peaceful and balanced environment
HEALTH maintaining physical and mental well-being	**HONESTY** being truthful and transparent in actions and words	**HUMILITY** valuing modesty and acknowledging one's limitations
INDEPENDENCE relying on oneself and making decisions autonomously	**INNER PEACE** achieving a state of mental and emotional tranquility	**INTEGRITY** upholding moral principles and honesty
KINDNESS showing generosity and consideration towards others	**LEARNING** continuously seeking knowledge and personal growth	**LOYALTY** being faithful and supportive to others

MINDFULNESS being present and fully engaged in the moment	**OPEN-MINDEDNESS** being receptive to new ideas and different perspectives	**PATIENCE** remaining calm and tolerant in challenging situations
PERSEVERANCE persisting in the face of difficulties	**POSITIVITY** maintaining an optimistic and hopeful attitude	**PURPOSE** living with intention and direction
RELIABILITY being dependable and consistent in actions	**RESILIENCE** bouncing back from adversity and maintaining strength	**RESPECT** valuing and honoring others
SELF-ACCEPTANCE embracing one's own worth and abilities	**SELF-CARE** prioritizing one's own well-being and health	**SELF-COMPASSION** treating oneself with kindness and understanding
SELF-DISCIPLINE exercising control over one's actions and impulses	**STABILITY** a sense of security, predictability, and steadiness in one's environment and life	**SIMPLICITY** seeing and appreciating the simple things in life
SUPPORTIVENESS providing help and encouragement to others	**TOLERANCE** accepting and respecting differences in others	**TRUST** believing in the reliability and integrity of others

<table>
<tr>
<td>WISDOM

applying knowledge and experience to make sound decisions</td>
<td>Add another value you want here…</td>
<td>Add another value you want here…</td>
</tr>
</table>

Step 2. Reflect. Take time to read each value and consider what it means to you personally. Reflect on how each value has played a role in your life and how it might help you manage anxiety.

Step 3. Sort. Sort the cards into three piles:

- **Very Important**: Values that resonate deeply with you and feel essential to your life.
- **Somewhat Important**: Values that matter to you but are not as crucial as the "Very Important" ones.
- **Less Important:** Values that are nice to cultivate but aren't critical to your sense of self or well-being.

Step 4. Prioritize. From the "Very Important" pile, choose your Top 5-10 values. These will be the core values that you can focus on to guide your actions and decisions.

Important: Of course, you're "Somewhat Important" and "Less Important" values are also critical. But just focus on your "Very Important" values for now so that you don't get overwhelmed. Once you get the hang of living according to your "Very Important" values, you can start exploring your other values using the steps in this exercise.

Step 5. Explore. Consider how each of your top values can help you manage your anxiety.

Example:
Mindfulness: Practicing mindfulness can help me stay present and hopefully reduce worries about the future.

Step 6. Accomplish. For each of your top values, write down at least three simple but specific actions to put the value into practice. For example:

Example: Mindfulness
- *Set aside 10 minutes each morning for mindfulness meditation.*
- *Do __Mindful Walking__ (page 61) every Saturday morning.*
- *List 3 things I'm grateful for at the end of each day.*

Step 7. Integrate. Make a conscious effort to incorporate your top values into your daily routines and decision-making processes. This alignment can help reduce anxiety by providing a sense of direction and purpose.

Step 8. Review and adjust. Every now and then, review your values and how they're influencing your life. Reflect on any changes and adjust your action plans to align with your core values.

Worksheet 23: Uncovering Values

Even though you might not have taken a moment to deeply reflect and identify your values (like what you did in the previous exercise), it doesn't mean you've never lived according to at least some of them. This exercise aims to "open your eyes" to values you may have already prioritized by reflecting on past events that have helped alleviate your anxiety.

Step 1. Reflect on past moments of anxiety relief. Think about a time when you felt relief from anxiety and experienced a sense of peace or fulfillment. What were you doing? What values do you think you were honoring in that moment?

Example: I remember feeling a sense of calm when I spent time gardening. The quiet and connection to nature eased my anxiety.

Step 2. Recall "decision points." Remember when you were faced with a decision during an anxious period. What guided you to make the choice you did? What values were at play?

*Example: I once chose between attending a high-stress social event (a colleague's gender reveal party) or staying home and reading a book about my anxiety disorder. I chose to stay home, valuing **self-care**, **growth**, and **peace** over social obligations. I think this is also about **authenticity** because I knew if I attended, I wouldn't just be anxious; I'd be "faking it" for hours for people I barely knew.*

Step 3. Envision your ideal self or your ideal life in an alternate universe. What are the most important things to you in that vision? What values do those things represent, especially in the context of managing anxiety?

Example: I see myself working in a peaceful environment, perhaps as a yoga instructor. This vision represents my values of tranquility, health, mindfulness, and balance.

Step 4. Optional: Think about your role models. If you want more insight, consider people you admire. What qualities do they have that you respect and want to emulate?

Example:
*My grandfather is my role model. To me, he was always a picture of **kindness**, **calmness**, **patience**, and **family**.*

Step 5. Optional: Consider what makes you anxious. If you want more insight, reflect on the past month. Reflect on situations that made you anxious. Often, anxiety arises when our values are violated or when you're not living in alignment with them.

Example:
Situation: I suffered an anxiety attack when I was told that I had to participate in a competitive work event designed to foster "team spirit" through a series of high-pressure games. I was in distress for weeks, anxious about performing well under stress and the social dynamics involved.
Reflection: Thinking about it now, I realize that my anxiety hinted that I was straying from my deeper values of calmness and inner peace. Also, I'm so not an extrovert so participating in the event and being "game" was making me feel like a fraud.
Values Identified: calmness, inner peace, personal authenticity

Situation:	
Reflection:	

Values Identified:

Step 6. Identify common themes. Reflect on your answers from the previous steps and look for common themes or patterns. These can give you clues about your personal values related to anxiety relief.

Example: I've noticed that most of my anxiety revolves around work (e.g., work performance, interaction with colleagues, social work events, etc.). I mostly get triggered there and bring the resulting anxiety with me everywhere throughout the day.

Step 7. Prioritize the values you've identified. Based on what feels most authentic and important, consider which values you want to prioritize in your daily life and decision-making, particularly in managing anxiety.

*Example: I realize that I want to prioritize **inner peace**. Looking back, I seek daily opportunities to create calm environments and practice relaxation techniques.*

Tip: Repeat this exercise to uncover more personal values.

Important: Prioritizing your values doesn't necessarily mean you need to overhaul your life (unless this is what you want to do). Focusing on your values can also mean making daily decisions, even small ones, according to these values. For example, if you value inner peace, you might create a quiet corner in your home for relaxation and mindfulness practices. You can level up later by integrating more substantial changes, like adopting a daily meditation routine.

Values vs. Goals

It's important to note that values are not the same as goals. Values are enduring principles that guide your behavior and give your life meaning. They're ongoing, continuous, and lived rather than achieved. For example, valuing *honesty* means striving to be authentic and truthful in ALL your interactions, regardless of the outcome. If you stop being honest, you no longer live by that value.

Conversely, goals are specific, achievable outcomes or targets you can "cross off." They're concrete and measurable; once achieved, you set new goals. So, a value is like a compass guiding your way; a goal is like a landmark you aim to reach as you follow that direction.

Although values and goals are different, they complement each other. Values provide direction and motivation, ensuring that your goals are meaningful and aligned with what truly matters to you. Goals give you tangible milestones to strive for, helping you to make progress and measure your success as you live according to your values.

If you feel that your current life goals aren't in alignment with your values, the following exercises will help you refine your objectives and ensure they truly reflect what's important to you.

Worksheet 24: Ikigai

Ikigai is a Japanese concept that means "reason for being." It's a philosophy that will help you find purpose and meaning in your life by identifying the intersection of four key elements: *what you love, what you are good at, what the world needs,* and *what you can be paid for.* When these elements align, they clarify your values and help you align your daily activities with your deeper purpose, reducing anxiety and uncertainty.

Step 1. Find a quiet place and sit comfortably. Take a few deep breaths to center yourself.

Step 2. Write down the things that you love doing. Think about activities that bring you joy and make you lose track of time. For example, "I love painting, spending time with my family, and helping others."

Step 3. Write down the things that you're good at. List your skills and strengths and where you excel, whether through natural talent or acquired skills. For example, "I'm good at art, creative thinking, and listening to others."

Step 4. Write down what you believe the world needs. This could be anything from more kindness and creativity to better mental health awareness. For example, "The world needs more empathy, less judgmental behavior, and better mental health support."

Step 5. Write down what you can be paid for. Consider your professional skills and how they can translate into a career or side project. For example, "I can be paid for art classes for kids and adults, art workshops, and maybe even designing websites."

Step 6. Find the intersection! Look for the overlaps among the four lists. Identify where your passions, skills, societal needs, and potential for income align. This is your Ikigai. For example, "My Ikigai seems to point to creating therapeutic art programs that help people manage anxiety through creative expression."

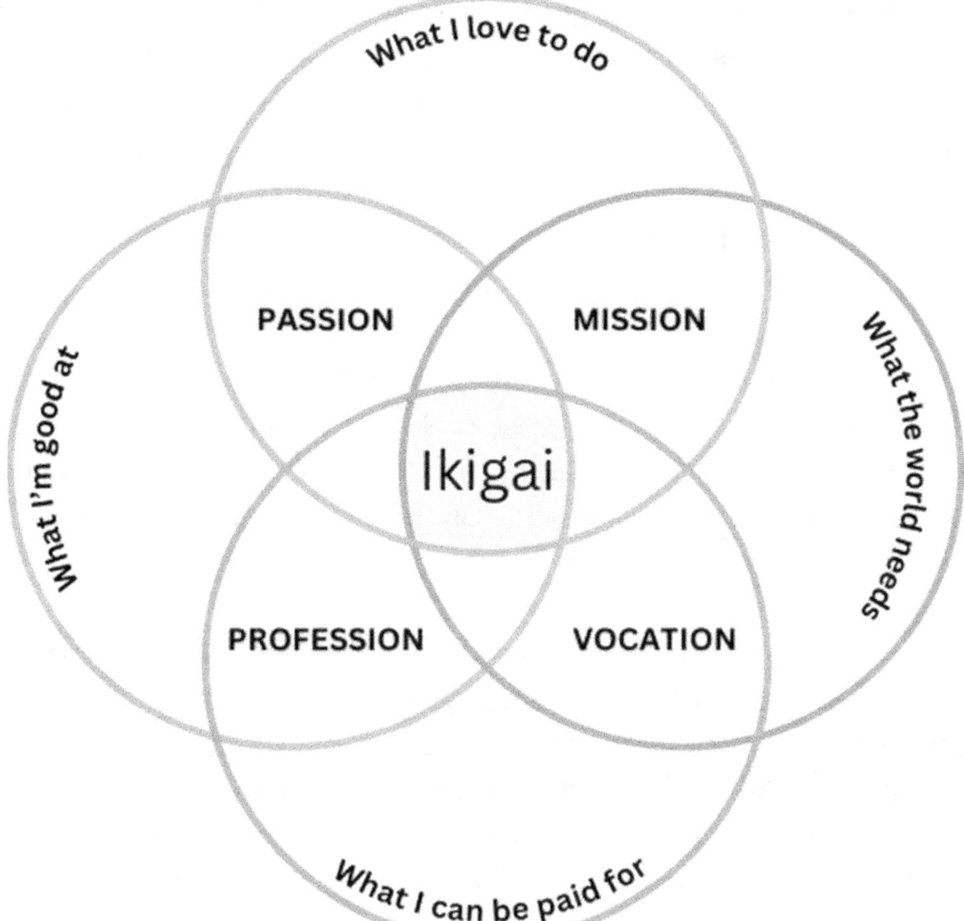

Step 7. Examine how your Ikigai aligns with your core values. Ask yourself if your Ikigai reflects what you believe in and what fulfills you. For example, "My core values of empathy, creativity, and mental health are reflected in my Ikigai of providing therapeutic art programs."

Step 8. Create a plan to integrate your Ikigai into your daily life. Set small, achievable goals that align with your Ikigai and help manage your anxiety. For example, "I will start by offering free weekly art therapy sessions in my community, gradually building up to a sustainable program."

Note: If you discover that your Ikigia, or life's purpose, doesn't align with your core values, it's time for some introspection and adjustment.

- **Reevaluate your Ikigai.** Sometimes, what you think is your Ikigai might be influenced by external pressures like societal expectations, family traditions, or financial needs rather than what truly brings us joy and fulfillment. Take time to reassess whether what you've identified in the previous steps truly resonates with what you want from life.

- **Modify your approach.** If your Ikigai is something you're passionate about but clashes with your values, consider ways to modify how you engage with this passion. For example, if you love your job but find that the competitive environment conflicts with your value of *calmness and inner peace*, look for ways to foster teamwork and community within your workplace. You can also seek other job opportunities where the atmosphere is not so cut-throat.

- **Seek balance!** Your life's purpose doesn't have to fulfill every aspect of your values. Find balance by integrating activities that reflect your values into your daily life, even if they are outside your primary Ikigai.

For example, suppose your Ikigai revolves around a high-pressure, demanding career in finance, which provides personal satisfaction through achievements and financial success. However, it doesn't fulfill other core values such as *service, supportiveness,* and *connection.* To achieve balance, you could integrate these values into your life by volunteering at local community centers on weekends or joining a group that organizes social events for underprivileged communities.

Worksheet 25: Value-Action Alignment

This exercise aims to help you identify your core values and ensure your daily actions align with these values.

Step 1. Reflect on what truly matters. Spend a few minutes reflecting on what is most important to you in different areas of your life (e.g., self, family, relationships, career, health, etc.). Think about moments when you felt truly fulfilled and content. What values were you honoring during those times?

Step 2. Review the <u>Discovering Values</u> exercise (page 112). Select the Top 3 values that resonate most with you in each life category. Next to each value, write down why that value is important to you.

Example:
Life Aspect: Self
Value #1: Authenticity. I want to be "myself." I think it will make me feel grounded and reduce the anxiety I feel from trying to be someone I'm not.
Value #2: Calmness. If I prioritize calmness, I can think more clearly and make better decisions, reducing the overall stress in my life.
Value #3: Growth. I'm anxious about the future. So, I think continuous personal growth will keep me motivated and help build my resilience and confidence.

Step 3. Action-value alignment. Rate how well your daily actions align with each value on a scale of 1 to 10 (with 1 being the lowest and 10 being the highest).

Life Aspect: Self

Value: Authenticity

Rating:

1	2	3	4	5	6	7	8	9	10

Life Aspect: Self

Value #1:

Rating:

1	2	3	4	5	6	7	8	9	10

Value #2:

Rating:

1	2	3	4	5	6	7	8	9	10

Value #3:

Rating:

1	2	3	4	5	6	7	8	9	10

Life Aspect: Family

Value #1:

Rating:

1	2	3	4	5	6	7	8	9	10

Value #2:

Rating:

1	2	3	4	5	6	7	8	9	10

Value #3:

Rating:

1	2	3	4	5	6	7	8	9	10

Life Aspect: Work/Career

Value #1:

Rating:

1	2	3	4	5	6	7	8	9	10

Value #2:									
Rating:									
1	2	3	4	5	6	7	8	9	10
Value #3:									
Rating:									
1	2	3	4	5	6	7	8	9	10

Note: Feel free to add more life aspects to your list and what values you want to rate.

Step 4. Identify gaps. Are you seeing gaps between your values and your actions?

Example: Yes. I rated the value of Authenticity as "2".

What specific actions are not in alignment?

Example: I still say "Yes" too often even though I don't want to, making me feel like a loser and a fraud often.

Step 5. Set goals. Write down specific, achievable goals to align your actions with your values. Write down at least one goal for each value.

Example: To be more authentic, I will say "No" to the first invitation I REALLY don't want to attend, no matter how hard the other person tries to persuade me.

Step 6. Develop an action plan. For each goal you listed above, write down the steps you must take to achieve it. Include resources or support you need, potential obstacles, and how you will overcome them.

Example: How to say "No."
- *I need to learn at least three ways to say "No" because saying a direct "No" is hard for me right now. For example, maybe I can sort of say "No" by offering an alternative? Something like, "I can't go with you guys to a bar tonight, but maybe next week?"*
- *Start with simple, low-stakes stuff like saying "No" when my corner barista offers to upgrade my order.*
- *Potential obstacle? My sister. We're close, and she means well, but she doesn't understand my anxiety about going home late. I need to be open (authentic!) and tell her about my anxiety over this.*

Conflicting Values

Real-life talk: I think some of my values are in conflict. Is that possible? It can definitely feel that way. For me, one of the values that I thought were in conflict was *independence* and *connection*. I value my independence and like making my own decisions, but I also value the deep connection I have with my husband. So, at first, I was a bit conflicted about it.

However, I realized I can balance these values by identifying which aspects I want to exert my independence on and which I need to prioritize connection.

First, I discussed this with my husband, so healthy communication was definitely important in this case. Ultimately, we agreed that for my independence, I would be free as a bird to pursue my hobbies and make personal decisions about my career.

For connection, we have date night every Tuesday (yes, Tuesday), where we focus on each other without distractions. Further, we must discuss and mutually agree (no independent decisions) on matters that affect us both.

If the previous exercises showed that you're having what seems like conflicting values, please do the following exercise to achieve balance and clarity.

Worksheet 26: Balancing Conflicting Values

Step 1. Identify the conflict. Write down the values that seem to be in conflict and reflect on why each value is important to you.

Example: Stability vs. Growth
Stability: I prefer routines, predictability, and safe environments because they help me manage my anxiety.
Growth: I want to explore new places and try new activities. I think trying to step out of my comfort zone and learning new things will help me.

Step 2. Communicate openly. Discuss your thoughts and feelings if other people are involved with keeping these values. You might also just want input from trusted friends or family members about your desire to balance these values. Share your concerns and aspirations and see what they think.

Step 3. Find common ground. Explore areas where the values can coexist.

Example: Stability vs. Growth
- *I'll start with small, manageable adventures that don't completely disrupt my routine.*
- *I ALWAYS stay home on Saturdays, so maybe I'll start by going out with a friend for breakfast or brunch on Saturday. This way, I can still go back to what I usually do when I return home.*

Step 4. Set boundaries. Establish limits on how much change you can handle, ensuring you can try new experiences while maintaining constancy.

Example: Stability vs. Growth
I'll only plan new activities during weekends to maintain a stable weekday routine.

Step 5. Small steps. Allow yourself to grow in small, manageable ways.

Example: I'll explore new things or visit new places WITHIN my city before planning any bigger trips. This way, my sense of stability is not threatened.

Step 6. Reflect and adjust. Regularly assess how well you're balancing these values. Make adjustments as needed to ensure both values are being honored.

Chapter 9: Committed Action

"It's not intentions that matter. It's actions. We are what we do and say, not what we intend to." – Anonymous

Committed Action is about taking concrete steps guided by your values, even in the face of difficult thoughts, feelings, or circumstances. It's about committing to behave in ways that align with your core values and sustain those behaviors over time despite challenges.

This ACT skill is important because you can identify your values and make plans to live by them, but if you don't continuously act on those plans, they remain intentions. **Committed action bridges the gap between understanding your values and living according to them.** It turns abstract values into concrete actions.

Key Components of Committed Action

- **Values-Guided.** Your behavior (actions) is constantly and purposefully driven by your personal values. For example, if you value health and well-being, you might commit to regular exercise and healthy eating, even when your anxiety tells you to stay in bed or reach for comfort food.

- **Flexibility.** Committed action involves being adaptable and flexible in your approach. It's about trying to live according to your values but not in a way that's resistant to change or the unexpected. For example, suppose you planned to attend a social event (value: connection) but felt overwhelmed with anxiety on the day. Instead of forcing yourself to go, you might decide to have a one-on-one coffee date with a close friend instead. This way, you still honor your value but adapt to your current emotional state.

- **Persistence.** Committed action requires perseverance and resilience. You must continuously take values-based action even when faced with obstacles or setbacks. For example, suppose you value *growth* in your work life or career. In this case, you might continue applying for new job opportunities despite experiencing anxiety over interviews or potential rejection. Each action taken, despite anxiety, demonstrates persistence toward your career goals.

- **Behavioral Change.** Committed action is *active*. It focuses on actual changes in behavior, not just changes in thoughts or feelings. It's about doing, not just thinking. For example, suppose you value *creativity*. Instead of just thinking about starting a new art project, you set aside time each day to paint or draw. Even if anxiety makes it hard to start, you focus on the *action* of creating art, leading to real behavioral change.

The following exercises are all designed to help you take committed steps to live and act according your core values—even in the face of internal resistance and life challenges.

Worksheet 27: WOOP!

WOOP stands for <u>W</u>ish, <u>O</u>utcome, <u>O</u>bstacle, and <u>P</u>lan. It's a goal-setting technique created by German psychologist Gabriele Oettingen.[43] It helps you visualize your goals, anticipate potential challenges, and create effective strategies to overcome them. WOOP can be particularly useful for managing anxiety, as it allows you to structure your thoughts and actions constructively. Linking it to your core values ensures that your actions are aligned with what truly matters to you.

Step 1. Identify your core values. Reflect on what's most important to you concerning your wish.

Step 2. Wish. Identify a meaningful and challenging goal related to your situation. This should be something that excites you, is important for your personal growth, and is aligned with your core values.

Step 3. Outcome. Visualize the best possible outcome if you achieve this goal. Think about how you would feel, what benefits you would gain, and how it would positively impact your life.

Step 4. Obstacle. Identify the main obstacles that might prevent you from achieving your goal. These could be internal (e.g., fears, habits, cognitive distortions, etc.) or external (e.g., finances, time constraints, knowledge, etc.).

Step 5. Plan. Develop a specific plan to overcome these obstacles. Create "if-then" statements to prepare for potential challenges.

RELATED VALUES:	*Example: self-care, connection, calmness, adaptability*
WISH	**My wish is to...** *Example:* *Smoothly transition to my new city and establish a sense*

of comfort and routine ASAP (preferably within three months).

As I relocate, I want to maintain self-care activities. I'm also anxious about being "uprooted," so I wish to build meaningful connections in my new place soon.

Everything will be new to me, which scares me, so I wish for calmness inside me and to demonstrate adaptability in my new surroundings.

OUTCOME

The best outcome for me is...

Example: A successful relocation. Achieving this will make me feel confident and happy. It also means I end up with a cozy home, a new social circle, and a good understanding of my new city.

OBSTACLE	**The potential obstacles are...** *Example: my anxiety, feeling homesick, struggling to make new friends, and dealing with the unfamiliarity of my new environment*
PLAN	**If... Then I will...** *Examples:* *Anxiety: If I experience anxiety, then I will practice deep breathing exercises, take a short walk to clear my mind, or use a grounding technique to bring myself back to the present moment.* *Self-Care: If I feel homesick, I will schedule regular video calls with my family and friends back home to maintain my emotional well-being.* *Connection: If I struggle to make new friends at work, I will join local clubs or groups that interest me. Maybe a book club, a sports team, or a Meetup group.*

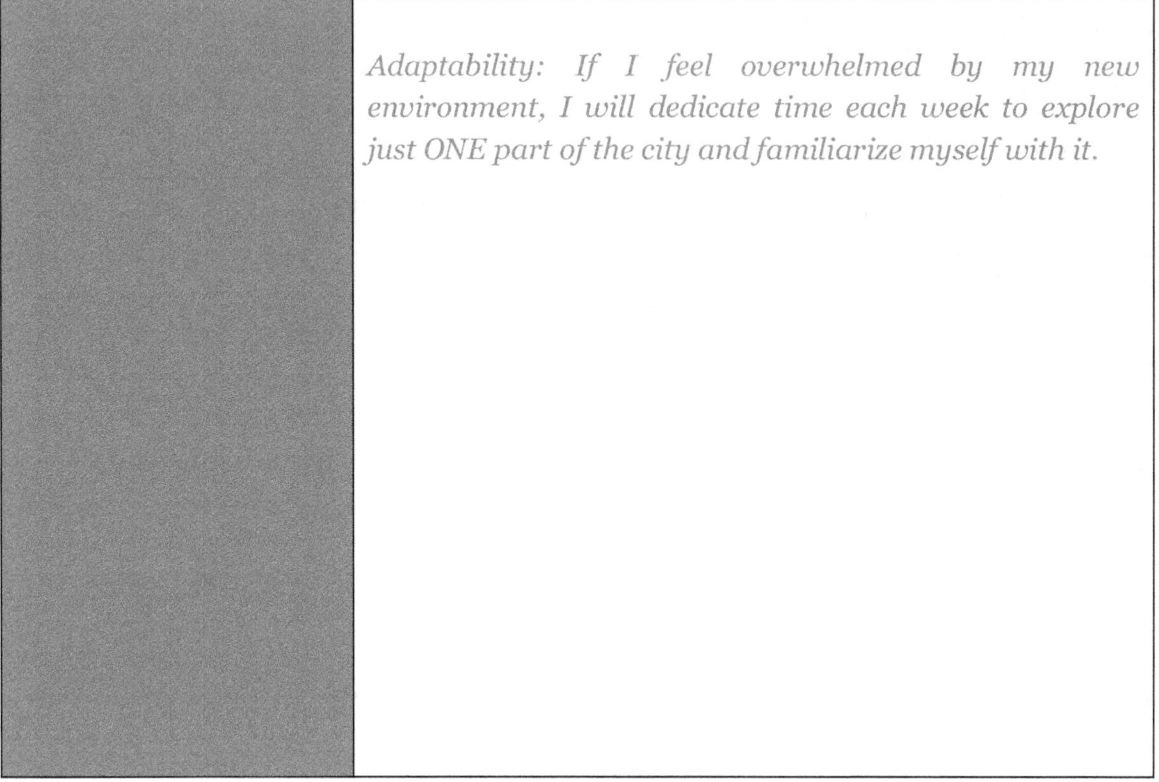

Adaptability: If I feel overwhelmed by my new environment, I will dedicate time each week to explore just ONE part of the city and familiarize myself with it.

Worksheet 28: Willingness Dial

Do this exercise whenever you are unwilling to act or accomplish a goal related to your values.

Step 1. Identify the challenging task or situation. Think about a task, goal, or situation you find challenging or currently avoiding. Also, identify why not doing this task goes against one of your core values.

Example:
Situation: Calling my parents to discuss my anxiety.
Violated Value: Authenticity

Step 2. Visualize a willingness dial. Close your eyes and take a few deep breaths to center yourself. Picture a dial in your mind, similar to a volume knob, labeled from 0 to 10, with 0 representing no willingness, while 10 represents full willingness to engage in the task or situation.

Ask yourself, "On a scale from 0 to 10, where is my current willingness to engage in this task?" Be honest with yourself and assign a number to your current level of willingness. For example, you might feel your willingness is at a "3."

Step 3. Explore the reasons behind your current willingness level. What thoughts, emotions, or physical sensations are influencing your willingness?

Example: I feel anxious about calling my parents and finally talking to them about my anxiety. I fear their disappointment and rejection; maybe they won't even believe me. I'm afraid to feel that vulnerable.

Step 4. Identify small steps to increase your willingness. Think about small, manageable steps that could increase your willingness by one or two points. These steps should be specific and doable.

Example: I can...
Practice mindfulness before the call, and prepare a script for the phone call.

Step 5. Commit to taking one small step. Choose one of the small steps you listed and commit to doing it. Write it down or say it out loud to reinforce your commitment. For example, "I will write a short script to guide my phone call and read it twice before dialing."

Step 6. Visualize moving the willingness dial. Close your eyes again and visualize moving the dial from your current number to one or two points higher. Imagine yourself feeling more willing and ready to engage in the task.

Picture yourself taking the small step you committed to and experiencing success.

Step 7. Take action. With the increased willingness you've just visualized, immediately dive into the task or situation without delay.

Worksheet 29: Acceptance and Commitment

This exercise will help you accept difficult emotions that might prevent you from doing value-driven actions.

Step 1. Identify the issue and related core value(s). Write down the specific issue you're dealing with and the affected value.

Example:
Issue: Thoughts like "I'm not good enough."
Affected value: self-care

Step 2. Write down any difficult emotions you're experiencing related to the issue. Be mindful and recognize your feelings without judgment.

Example: When thoughts like "I'm not good enough" enter my mind, I feel depressed and overwhelmed because I feel like they're preventing me from practicing self-care.

Step 3. Accept your emotions AS IS. Practice accepting your emotions instead of trying to avoid or suppress them. Understand that it's okay to feel this way and emotions are a natural part of life.

Example: I accept that feeling sadness and anxiety due to "I'm not good enough" thoughts are normal. It's okay to feel this way. I don't need to fight these feelings.

Step 4. Define value-driven actions. After accepting your difficult emotions, determine actions that align with your core values as best as possible.

Examples:
- If thoughts of not being good enough enter my mind, I'll practice mindfulness and *STOP (page **Error! Bookmark not defined.**).*
- I will practice self-compassion by writing three positive things about myself every morning.
- I will dedicate 30 minutes each day to an activity that I enjoy, and that relaxes me, like reading a book or walking in nature.

Step 5. Commit to action. Plan when and how to carry out the actions you listed in the previous step.

Example:
Action: I will dedicate 30 minutes each day to an activity that I enjoy and relaxes me, like reading a book or walking in nature.
Commitment: I will schedule this time as a non-negotiable appointment on my calendar.

Worksheet 30: Behavioral Activation

Committed action is "values in motion." This exercise will help you focus on activities that promote living according to your values.

Step 1. List one core value, specify a goal related to this value, and outline activities you can do within one week to achieve this goal.

Example:

Values: initiative

Goal: Be the one to reach out to others and not wait for others to contact me first.

Activities: Call a friend or family member to catch up. Ask a colleague or acquaintance to plan a coffee or lunch meeting.

Step 2. Schedule activities. Plan when and how you will engage in these activities. Schedule them realistically within your week to ensure you can commit to them.

Example:

Monday: Call a friend in the evening.

Tuesday: Email a colleague to arrange a coffee meeting.

Wednesday: Text a family member to check in and chat.

Thursday: Send a message to an old friend to reconnect.

Friday: Approach a coworker and ask if they want to have lunch together.

Important: Please DO NOT be discouraged if you receive a "No" or if things don't go as you hoped or planned. The important thing is to start and continue your efforts!

Step 3. Reflect. After completing each activity, take some time to reflect on how it impacted your mood and how it aligned with your values. Write down your thoughts and feelings.

Example: Calling a friend on Monday made me feel happy and less alone.

Worksheet 31: FEAR

Committed action involves taking effective action guided by your values, even in the presence of difficult thoughts and emotions. The FEAR exercise (Fusion, Excessive goals, Avoidance of discomfort, and Remoteness from values) helps you break free from patterns that might be preventing you from living a life aligned with your values.

Step 1. Identify a core value and related goal you're finding hard to live by.

Example:
Value: Health
Goal: Start and stick to a regular exercise routine to improve my physical and mental well-being.

Step 2. Recognize FEAR patterns. Complete the FEAR table below to identify the thoughts, goals, behaviors, and beliefs that might prevent you from committing to your core values.

Fusion: When you become entangled (fused) with your negative thinking patterns and believe them as absolute truths.

Excessive goals: When your objectives are too high or unachievable given your present circumstances or resources.

Avoidance of discomfort: When you steer clear of situations that cause anxiety or stress.

<u>R</u>emoteness from values: When you lose touch with WHY this core value is important to you.

Value:	*Example: Health*
Goal:	*Example: Start and stick to a regular exercise routine to improve my physical and mental well-being.*
<u>F</u>usion	**What thoughts are making you think your goal is unachievable?** *Example: I'm too out of shape to even start exercising. I've tried before, and I'll probably fail again.*
<u>E</u>xcessive goals	**What goal(s) might be "too much" or exceeding your current resources (e.g., skills, time, money, etc.)?** *Example: I want to work out for one solid hour daily, or it's*

<table>
<tr>
<td></td>
<td>not worth it. This may be unrealistic because I'm just starting, and my workload is currently high.</td>
</tr>
<tr>
<td>Avoidance of discomfort</td>
<td>What discomfort are you avoiding?

Example: I think I'm avoiding exercising because it's too physically uncomfortable and tiring. Also, time-wise, one hour of exercising out of my schedule is inconvenient.</td>
</tr>
<tr>
<td>Remoteness from values</td>
<td>Are you perhaps losing touch with or forgetting what is important or meaningful about this goal?

Example: I guess I'm too focused on how hard this goal is, and I forget why prioritizing my well-being matters.</td>
</tr>
</table>

Worksheet 32: Reflection and Recommitment

Challenges, obstacles, setbacks... they're all part of life. So, it's possible that despite your best efforts, you find yourself "veering off track" of your outlined committed actions to live a value-based life. This exercise will help you understand why you deviated from your plans and how to recommit to them.

Step 1. Find a quiet place where you can reflect without distractions. Take a few deep breaths to center yourself.

Step 2. Reflect on your day and identify moments when you failed to live according to your values.

What happened today that made you feel you failed to live by your values?

Example: Today, I was short, grumpy, and dismissive with a colleague when they asked for help. This behavior goes against my values of being supportive and kind.

How did you feel during those moments?

Example: I felt frustrated and impatient, which made me snap at them. Afterward, I felt guilty and disappointed in myself for not being more understanding.

Step 3. Identify triggers. Think about what triggered you to act in a way that wasn't aligned with your values.

What specific events or emotions led to your actions?

Example: I was feeling overwhelmed with my own workload. When my colleague interrupted me, it triggered feelings of stress and impatience.

Were there any external pressures or internal thoughts that influenced your behavior?

Example: The external pressure of looming deadlines contributed to my stress. Internally, I thought I didn't have time to help others, making me react negatively.

Step 4. Consider the impact of your actions on yourself and others.

How did acting against your values affect your mood, stress levels, and relationships?

Example: Acting against my values increased my stress because I was dwelling on my reaction. It also strained my relationship with my colleague, making me worry about how they perceive me.

What consequences did you notice?

Example: My colleague seemed annoyed and less willing to approach me afterward, which could lead to a breakdown in our teamwork. Additionally, I felt more stressed and guilty, which affected my focus for the rest of the day.

Step 5. Recommit to your values. Write down your core values and why they are important to you. Make a commitment to realign your actions with your values moving forward.

List at least three core values, and why do they matter to you?

Example:

Kindness*: Being kind is important to me because it fosters positive relationships and a supportive environment.*

Patience*: Patience helps me respond thoughtfully rather than react impulsively, which is essential for maintaining balance and harmony in my interactions.*

Integrity*: Acting with integrity ensures I stay true to my principles, even in challenging situations.*

How can you ensure your actions align with these values tomorrow?

Example: Tomorrow, I will remind myself to take a deep breath before responding to anyone, ensuring I approach them with kindness and patience. I'll also prioritize my tasks to avoid feeling overwhelmed and maintain my integrity by being honest about my availability.

Step 6. Set specific actions. Identify specific actions you can take tomorrow to live according to your values. Remember, a plan without action is just *intention*.

What specific steps will you take <u>tomorrow</u> to honor your values?
Example:
I will set aside time in the morning to plan my day, ensuring I have a clear idea of what needs to be done.

I'll practice mindfulness during my breaks to keep my stress levels in check.
I'll approach my colleague first thing in the morning to apologize and offer my help when I'm less busy.

How will you handle similar triggers or situations differently?

Example: If I feel overwhelmed again, I'll take a moment to breathe and assess the situation calmly before responding (mindfulness!). I'll remind myself that being supportive and kind is more important than the immediate task, and I can find a balance between helping others and managing my responsibilities.

Conclusion

Anxiety. I've suffered from it for years, so I have a pretty good idea of just how much pain you're carrying right now. However, I realized I can lighten the mental, emotional, and often physical load I carry. I can get better and experience anxiety relief. Contrary to popular belief, though, it's not as simple as deciding to put down that "load." (If only it was THAT easy!)

The door to anxiety relief starts to open when you realize and decide you need help. Your decision to get this book marks the beginning of your journey, but it's the consistent and committed actions that will truly make a difference!

Acceptance and Commitment Therapy (ACT) teaches you that rather than battling anxiety, you can accept its presence without letting it dictate your life. By practicing the skills in this book and developing *psychological flexibility*, you can slowly but surely loosen the grip that anxiety has on you.

Remember, relief doesn't come from eliminating anxiety entirely but from changing your relationship with it. It's about learning to carry your load in a way that feels lighter, even on the toughest days.

So, take that first step, then another, and keep moving forward. Relief is possible, and it starts with acceptance, commitment, and the courage to live a life true to your values.

A Little Help?

"In helping others, we shall help ourselves, for whatever good we give out completes the circle and comes back to us." — Flora Edwards

Writing this book has been a personal journey for me. Anxiety. Wow. It's very hard to explain to people who haven't experienced it, isn't it? So, I sincerely hope you find a friend or ally in this book. That there's something on these pages that can help you. And above all, I wish you relief from your anxiety and pain.

Many people don't realize just how hard it is to get reviews and how much they help us authors. So, I would be incredibly grateful if you could take just a few seconds to write a short review about this book on Amazon.

How to Help
Step 1. Please visit this link
https://tinyurl.com/act4anxiety or scan the QR code on this page.
Step 2. Share your thoughts about this book on Amazon (60-90 seconds).
Step 3. Thank you. You have helped!

Note: If you're from outside the US, please update the link above from amazon.com to your country code (e.g., amazon.co.uk, amazon.ca, amazon.de, etc.).

Using Kindle or an e-reader? Scroll to the bottom of the book and swipe up to prompt the Review page.

THANK YOU FOR YOUR HELP!

Further Reading...

If you're struggling with practicing Acceptance and want help from someone who knows exactly what you're going through, please let me share my journey with you through this Amazon bestselling resource.

The Radical Acceptance Workbook

Transform Your Life & Free Your Mind with the Healing Power of Self-Love & Compassion — Positive Lessons to Treat Anxiety, Self-Doubt, Shame & Negative Self-Judgement

Click this link: https://amzn.to/3XXuiGI
Or scan the QR code on this page.

The ACT Therapy Workbook for Adults

An Easy-to-Read (No Jargon!) Acceptance & Commitment Therapy Guide for Mindfulness and Mental Wellness

Deepen your understanding of Acceptance and Commitment Therapy (ACT) in general (not just for anxiety relief). Get it for yourself or as a thoughtful gift for someone navigating their own mental health challenges.

Visit this link: https://amzn.to/3WMsnUC
Or scan the QR code on this page.

The Perfect Gift for Tweens & Teens

DBT Skills Workbook for Teens

A Fun and Highly Relatable Workbook for Teens to Manage Difficult Emotions, Cope with Teen Stress & Create Better Friendships

Includes 60+ Engaging Worksheets!

Click here to get your DBT copy now:
https://amzn.to/3BJcQyg
Or scan the QR code on this page.

About the Author

Ava Walters is the founder of LifeZen Publications. Coming from a family with a history of mental health issues, her journey began as a personal quest to find balance, inner peace, and what we all desire—happiness. This pursuit has led her to explore traditional psychotherapeutic methods and diverse holistic practices.

She has an MBA with a specialization in International Project Management (IPM). However, her trajectory took a significant turn after experiencing "a burnout and a breakdown." She then returned to her first love—writing, complementing it with her deep passion for psychology. This transformation marked the beginning of her new journey. One focused on unraveling the intricate connections between human behavior and mental healing.

When she's not writing, Ava can be found on her yoga mat, taking long nature walks with her husband, or in the kitchen, constantly experimenting with new recipes to her husband's delight.

Learn more about Ava and LifeZen Publications here:
https://life-zen.com/

Index

References

1 Linehan, M. M. (University of W., USA). (2014). *DBT (R) skills training manual, Second Edition.* Guilford Publications.

2 Walters, A. (2024). *The Radical Acceptance Workbook* (Ser. Acceptance Therapy). LifeZen Publications.

3 Mah, L., Szabuniewicz, C., & Fiocco, A. J. (2016). Can anxiety damage the brain? *Current Opinion in Psychiatry, 29*(1), 56–63. https://doi.org/10.1097/yco.0000000000000223

4 Staner, L. (2003). Sleep and anxiety disorders. *Dialogues in Clinical Neuroscience, 5*(3), 249–258. https://doi.org/10.31887/dcns.2003.5.3/lstaner

5 *Obesity and anxiety disorder: Which one comes first?.* Obesity Medicine Association. (n.d.). https://obesitymedicine.org/blog/obesity-and-anxiety-disorder-which-one-comes-first/

6 Abraham, M. (2020, October 10). *Can anxiety cause weight gain?.* Calm Clinic - Information about Anxiety, Stress and Panic. https://www.calmclinic.com/anxiety/symptoms/weight-gain

7 Cherney, K. (2023, November 13). *Effects of anxiety on the body.* Healthline. https://www.healthline.com/health/anxiety/effects-on-body

8 Ross, R. A., Foster, S. L., & Ionescu, D. F. (2017). The role of chronic stress in anxious depression. *Chronic Stress, 1,* 2470547016689472. https://doi.org/10.1177/2470547016689472

9 Kalin, N. H. (2020). The critical relationship between anxiety and depression. *American Journal of Psychiatry, 177*(5), 365–367. https://doi.org/10.1176/appi.ajp.2020.20030305

10 *Anxiety and heart disease.* Johns Hopkins Medicine. (2023, October 30). https://www.hopkinsmedicine.org/health/conditions-and-diseases/anxiety-and-heart-disease

11 Ferguson, S. (2024, July 23). *Anxiety treatment: Self-help, therapy, medication.* Healthline. https://www.healthline.com/health/anxiety-treatment
Medically reviewed by Joslyn Jelinek, LCSW, ACSW, RDDP.

12 American Psychiatric Association. (2022). *Anxiety disorders.* Diagnostic and statistical manual of mental disorders (5th ed., text rev., pp. 215-231). American Psychiatric Association.

13 Booth, J. (2023, October 23). *Anxiety statistics and facts.* Forbes. https://www.forbes.com/health/mind/anxiety-statistics/
Expert Reviewed by Sabrina Romanoff, Psy.D. Psychology.

14 U.S. Department of Health and Human Services. (n.d.). *Social anxiety disorder.* National Institute of Mental Health. https://www.nimh.nih.gov/health/statistics/social-anxiety-disorder

15 Thompson, B. (2024, April 22). *Exploring the recent rise of Social Anxiety Disorder - Seattle psychiatrist.* Seattle Anxiety Specialists - Psychiatry, Psychology, and Psychotherapy. https://seattleanxiety.com/psychiatrist/2023/2/24/exploring-the-recent-rise-of-social-anxiety-disorder

16 Mayo Foundation for Medical Education and Research. (2018, May 4). *Anxiety disorders*. Mayo Clinic. https://www.mayoclinic.org/diseases-conditions/anxiety/symptoms-causes/syc-20350961

17 Spitzer, R. L., Kroenke, K., Williams, J. B., & Löwe, B. (2006). A brief measure for assessing generalized anxiety disorder. *Archives of Internal Medicine, 166*(10), 1092. https://doi.org/10.1001/archinte.166.10.1092

18 Cohen, S., Kamarck, T., & Mermelstein, R. (1983). Perceived stress scale. *PsycTESTS Dataset.* https://doi.org/10.1037/t02889-000

19 *Women are more than twice as likely to develop anxiety disorders.* University of Utah Health | University of Utah Health. (2023, August 15). https://healthcare.utah.edu/the-scope/health-library/all/2016/12/women-are-more-twice-likely-develop-anxiety-disorders

20 Remes, O., Brayne, C., van der Linde, R., & Lafortune, L. (2016). A systematic review of reviews on the prevalence of anxiety disorders in adult populations. *Brain and Behavior, 6*(7). https://doi.org/10.1002/brb3.497

21 McLean, C. P., Asnaani, A., Litz, B. T., & Hofmann, S. G. (2011). Gender differences in anxiety disorders: Prevalence, course of illness, comorbidity and burden of illness. *Journal of Psychiatric Research, 45*(8), 1027–1035. https://doi.org/10.1016/j.jpsychires.2011.03.006

22 Wieczorek, K., Targonskaya, A., & Maslowski, K. (2023). Reproductive hormones and female mental wellbeing. *Women, 3*(3), 432–444. https://doi.org/10.3390/women3030033

23 *Menopause and your mental wellbeing*. NHS inform. (2022, November 29). https://www.nhsinform.scot/healthy-living/womens-health/later-years-around-50-years-and-over/menopause-and-post-menopause-health/menopause-and-your-mental-wellbeing/

24 *Men's Mental Health*. Men's Mental Health | Anxiety and Depression Association of America, ADAA. (n.d.). https://adaa.org/find-help/by-demographics/mens-mental-health

25 Thomas, D. (2024, May 3). *Why are men less likely to get mental health help?*. The Walker Center. https://www.thewalkercenter.org/blog-posts/why-are-men-less-likely-to-get-mental-health-help

26 Keyes, K. M., McLaughlin, K. A., Vo, T., Galbraith, T., & Heimberg, R. G. (2015). Anxious and aggressive: The co-occurrence of IED with anxiety disorders. *Depression and Anxiety*, *33*(2), 101–111. https://doi.org/10.1002/da.22428

27 Hawkins, K. A., & Cougle, J. R. (2010). Anger problems across the anxiety disorders: Findings from a population-based study. *Depression and Anxiety*, *28*(2), 145–152. https://doi.org/10.1002/da.20764

28 *About*. Steven C. Hayes, PhD. (2024, June 10). https://stevenchayes.com/about/

29 Khoury, B., Lecomte, T., Fortin, G., Masse, M., Therien, P., Bouchard, V., Chapleau, M.-A., Paquin, K., & Hofmann, S. G. (2013). Mindfulness-based therapy: A comprehensive meta-analysis. *Clinical Psychology Review*, *33*(6), 763–771. https://doi.org/10.1016/j.cpr.2013.05.005

30 Mindful Staff. (2022, August 31). *The science of mindfulness.* Mindful.
https://www.mindful.org/the-science-of-mindfulness/

31 Isbel, B., Weber, J., Lagopoulos, J., Stefanidis, K., Anderson, H., &
Summers, M. J. (2020). Neural changes in early visual processing after
6 months of mindfulness training in older adults. *Scientific Reports,*
10(1). https://doi.org/10.1038/s41598-020-78343-w

32 Jha, A. P., Krompinger, J., & Baime, M. J. (2007). Mindfulness training
modifies subsystems of attention. *Cognitive, affective & behavioral*
neuroscience, 7(2), 109–119. https://doi.org/10.3758/cabn.7.2.109

33 Roemer, L., Williston, S. K., & Rollins, L. G. (2015). Mindfulness and
emotion regulation. *Current Opinion in Psychology, 3,* 52–57.
https://doi.org/10.1016/j.copsyc.2015.02.006

34 Heppner, W. L., Spears, C. A., Vidrine, J. I., & Wetter, D. W. (2015).
Mindfulness and emotion regulation. *Handbook of Mindfulness and Self-*
Regulation, 107–120. https://doi.org/10.1007/978-1-4939-2263-5_9

35 Liu, T. (2018). The scientific hypothesis of an "energy system" in the human
body. *Journal of Traditional Chinese Medical Sciences, 5*(1), 29–34.
https://doi.org/10.1016/j.jtcms.2018.02.003

36 Collins, N. (2018, June 11). *How the human mind shapes reality.* Stanford
Report. https://news.stanford.edu/stories/2018/06/four-ways-human-
mind-shapes-reality

37 Vilhauer, J. (2020, September 27). *How your thinking creates your reality.*
Psychology Today. https://www.psychologytoday.com/intl/blog/living-

forward/202009/how-your-thinking-creates-your-reality

Reviewed by Lybi Ma

38 Hampton, D. (2022, October 24). *Science proves your thoughts influence your reality and shape your brain for better or worse. you choose.* The Best Brain Possible. https://thebestbrainpossible.com/thoughts-brain-neuroplasticity-reality/

39 Kosslyn, S. M., & Thompson, W. L. (2003). When is early visual cortex activated during visual mental imagery? *Psychological Bulletin, 129*(5), 723–746. https://doi.org/10.1037/0033-2909.129.5.723

40 Morewedge, C. K., Huh, Y. E., & Vosgerau, J. (2010). Thought for food: Imagined consumption reduces actual consumption. *Science, 330*(6010), 1530–1533. https://doi.org/10.1126/science.1195701

41 Blanco, A.-L. (2020, April 2). *Our brain doesn't tell the difference between simulation and Reality.* SkillGym. https://www.skillgym.com/2019/05/our-brain-doesnt-tell-the-difference-between-simulation-and-reality/

42 Dijkstra, N., & Fleming, S. M. (2023). Subjective signal strength distinguishes reality from imagination. *Nature Communications, 14*(1). https://doi.org/10.1038/s41467-023-37322-1

43 Wikimedia Foundation. (2024, June 8). *Gabriele Oettingen.* Wikipedia. https://en.wikipedia.org/wiki/Gabriele_Oettingen